Gothic Classics

Graphic Classics Volume Fourteen

2007

Edited by Tom Pomplun

EUREKA PRODUCTIONS

8778 Oak Grove Road, Mount Horeb, Wisconsin 53572
www.graphicclassics.com

I'VE A PAIN IN MY HEAD

a poem by **Jane Austen** · *illustrated by* **Molly Kiely**

ILLUSTRATIONS ©2007 MOLLY KIELY

EDITOR'S NOTE: CALOMEL BRISK WAS A COMMON 19TH-CENTURY PURGATIVE.

CONTENTS

Gothic Classics
Graphic Classics Volume Fourteen

©2007 ANNE TIMMONS

I've a Pain in my Head
by Jane Austen, illustrated by Molly Kiely 2

Carmilla
by Joseph Sheridan Le Fanu, adapted by Rod Lott, illustrated by Lisa K. Weber 4

The Mysteries of Udolpho
by Ann Radcliffe, adapted by Antonella Caputo, illustrated by Carlo Vergara 44

The Oval Portrait
by Edgar Allan Poe, adapted by Tom Pomplun, illustrated by Leong Wan Kok 90

Northanger Abbey
by Jane Austen, adapted by Trina Robbins, illustrated by Anne Timmons 94

At the Gate
by Myla Jo Closser, adapted by Tom Pomplun, illustrated by Shary Flenniken 134

About the Artists & Writers 142

Cover illustration by Lisa K. Weber / Back cover illustration by Trina Robbins

Gothic Classics: Graphic Classics Volume Fourteen / ISBN13 #978-0-9787919-0-2 / ISBN10 #0-9787919-0-8 is published by Eureka Productions. Price US $11.95, CAN $14.50. Available from Eureka Productions, 8778 Oak Grove Road, Mount Horeb, WI 53572. Tom Pomplun, designer and publisher, tom@graphicclassics.com. Eileen Fitzgerald, editorial assistant. Compilation and all original works ©2007 Eureka Productions. Graphic Classics is a trademark of Eureka Productions. For ordering information and previews of upcoming volumes visit the Graphic Classics website at http://www.graphicclassics.com. Printed in Canada.

J. Sheridan LeFanu's

Carmilla

adapted by
Rod Lott

art by
Lisa K. Weber

My father was English, and I bear an
English name. But here, in lonely and
primitive Styria, we inhabited a castle.

He was in the Austrian service and
retired upon a pension, purchasing this
feudal residence and the small estate
on which it stands.

Nothing could be more picturesque. . . or more solitary.

At the time of my story, I was only eighteen. My father and I constituted the family, along with the servants.

Mme. Perrodon, my governess, whose care supplied to me the loss of my mother.

Mlle. De Lafontaine, my finishing governess.

One of the very earliest incidents of my life which I can recollect produced a terrible impression upon my mind, which never has been effaced.

I can't have been more than six years old when one night I awoke and failed to see the nursery maid.

I was vexed at being neglected, but to my surprise, I saw a pretty face looking at me. I gazed at her in wonder and ceased whimpering.

The girl lay beside me, smiling. I felt immediately soothed and fell asleep again.

OH!

I was awakened by a sensation as if two needles ran deep into my breast.

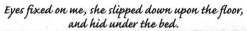

*Eyes fixed on me, she slipped down upon the floor,
and hid under the bed.*

HELP ME!

Mme. Perrodon and the
housekeeper came running in.
I saw their faces were pale as
they looked about the room.

LAY YOUR HAND ALONG THAT
HOLLOW. SOMEONE *DID* LIE THERE.
THE PLACE IS STILL WARM!

SHE HURT ME HERE.

THERE'S NO VISIBLE
SIGN THAT ANYTHING
HAPPENED, DEAR.

DON'T BE
FRIGHTENED. IT
WAS NOTHING BUT A
DREAM AND CAN'T
HURT YOU.

But I was not comforted.

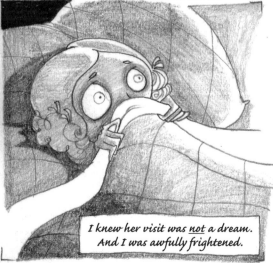

*I knew her visit was <u>not</u> a dream.
And I was awfully frightened.*

6

Twelve years later, the memory still haunted me.

GENERAL SPIELSDORF AND HIS NIECE CAN'T COME VISIT TOMORROW AS WE HAD HOPED.

HOW SOON *SHALL* THEY COME?

NOT 'TIL AUTUMN. I'M GLAD NOW YOU NEVER KNEW MADEMOISELLE RHEINFELDT.

WHY?

BECAUSE THE POOR YOUNG LADY IS *DEAD.*

HERE'S HIS LETTER...

I'M AFRAID HE'S IN GREAT AFFLICTION.

I've lost my darling daughter, for as such I loved her. The fiend who entered our house and betrayed our hospitality has done it all.

I thank God my child died without knowing the nature of her illness.

I devote my remaining days to tracking this monster. Pray for me, dear friend.

General Spielsdorf

We were speculating upon the possible meanings of those sentences, when we met Mme. Perrodon and Mlle. De Lafontaine, who had come out to enjoy the exquisite moonlight.

The unwonted sound of carriage wheels and many hooves upon the road arrested our attention. It seemed to be carrying a person of rank.

Approaching the drawbridge, it swerved, bringing a wheel over the roots of a huge lime tree by the road.

HEAVENS!

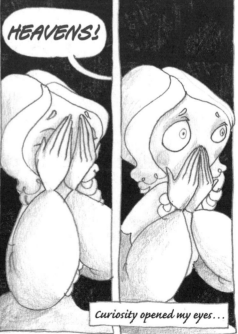

I knew what was coming. I covered my eyes, and heard a cry from my companions.

Curiosity opened my eyes...

...and I saw a scene of utter confusion.

SHE IS STUNNED, NOT DEAD.

WHO WAS *EVER* SO BORN TO CALAMITY? HERE I AM, ON A JOURNEY OF LIFE AND DEATH, IN WHICH TO LOSE AN *HOUR* IS POSSIBLY TO LOSE ALL!

MY CHILD WILL *NOT* RECOVER IN TIME. HOW FAR IS THE NEAREST VILLAGE? I MUST LEAVE HER THERE FOR THREE MONTHS!

OH, PAPA, ASK HER TO LET HER STAY WITH US!

IF MADAME WILL ENTRUST HER TO THE CARE OF MY DAUGHTER AND HER GOVERNESS...

I CANNOT DO THAT, SIR.. IT WOULD TASK YOUR CHIVALRY TOO CRUELLY.

ON THE CONTRARY. MY DAUGHTER HAS JUST BEEN DISAPPOINTED BY A CRUEL MISFORTUNE. TO CONFIDE THIS YOUNG LADY TO OUR CARE WILL BE HER BEST CONSOLATION.

Out of my hearing, she talked to him with a stern countenance. I was curious to learn what she was speaking with so much rapidity.

But then she turned to her daughter, and whispered in her ear...

...then stepped into her carriage, which whirled away.

Nothing remained but the young lady, who at that moment opened her eyes.

WHERE IS MAMA?

WHERE AM I?

WHAT *IS* THIS PLACE?

WHERE IS MY MOTHER?

I wanted to add my consolations.

DON'T APPROACH NOW.. A VERY LITTLE EXCITEMENT WOULD POSSIBLY OVERPOWER HER..

That night, we talked over the adventure of the evening.

SHE'S THE PRETTIEST CREATURE I EVER SAW— SO GENTLE AND POLITE.

ABSOLUTELY BEAUTIFUL!

AND SUCH A SWEET VOICE!

DID YOU SEE WHAT AN ILL-LOOKING PACK OF MEN THE SERVANTS WERE?

UGLY, HANG-DOG LOOKING FELLOWS. I HOPE THEY MAY NOT ROB THE POOR LADY IN THE FOREST!

THEIR FACES WERE STRANGELY LEAN, AND DARK, AND SULLEN.

I'M CURIOUS....

...BUT I DARE SAY THE YOUNG LADY WILL TELL YOU ABOUT IT TOMORROW.

I DON'T THINK SHE WILL.

That made us all the more curious as to what had passed between him and the lady...

I entreated him to tell me.

SHE EXPRESSED HER RELUCTANCE TO TROUBLE US, THEN SAID, "I AM ON A LONG JOURNEY OF VITAL IMPORTANCE, RAPID AND SECRET."

SHE SAID, "I SHALL RETURN IN THREE MONTHS."

I HOPE I HAVE NOT DONE A FOOLISH THING.

I LONG TO SEE AND TALK TO HER.

The doctor did not arrive until nearly 1 o'clock. I was too excited to sleep.

The physician reported very favorably on his patient. She was sitting up, apparently perfectly well.

HELLO, MY
NAME IS L—

What was it that made me recoil? I saw the very face which had visited me in my childhood, which I had for years ruminated with horror!

THE DOCTOR THINKS YOU OUGHT TO HAVE A MAID SIT WITH YOU TONIGHT.

HOW KIND, BUT I HAVE A TERROR OF ROBBERS, SO I ALWAYS LOCK MY DOOR.

GOODNIGHT, DEAR FRIEND.

I THINK WE SHALL BE CLOSE FRIENDS. SHE IS THE MOST BEAUTIFUL CREATURE I'VE EVER SEEN.

I was charmed with her in most particulars. There were some that did not please me so well. She exercised an ever-wakeful reserve with respect to everything in her life.

What she did tell me amounted, in my estimation, to nothing...

FIRST: HER NAME IS CARMILLA.

SECOND: HER FAMILY IS ANCIENT AND NOBLE.

THIRD: HER HOME LAY IN THE WEST.

WHY WON'T YOU TELL ME THE NAME OF YOUR FAMILY – YOUR ESTATE – YOUR COUNTRY?

DEAREST, THINK ME NOT CRUEL BECAUSE I OBEY THE IRRESISTIBLE LAW OF MY STRENGTH AND WEAKNESS.

AS I DRAW NEAR TO YOU, YOU, IN YOUR TURN, WILL DRAW NEAR TO OTHERS, AND LEARN THE RAPTURE OF THAT CRUELTY WHICH YET IS LOVE.

Her murmured words sounded like a lullaby in my ear, soothing my resistance into a trance.

IN THESE MYSTERIOUS MOODS, I DO NOT LIKE HER.

I experienced pleasurable excitement, mingled with fear and disgust; adoration and abhorrence. This, I know, is paradox, but I cannot explain the feeling.

She sometimes alluded to her home, indicating a people of strange customs. I gathered from these chance hints her native country was more remote than I had first imagined.

THAT POOR GIRL FANCIED SHE SAW A GHOST A FORTNIGHT AGO, AND HAS BEEN DYING EVER SINCE. SHE EXPIRED YESTERDAY.

HOW DISCORDANT THEIR VOICES ARE!

16

ON THE CONTRARY, I THINK THEIR SINGING VERY *SWEET*.

I *HATE* FUNERALS! WHAT A FUSS! *EVERYONE* MUST DIE, AND ALL ARE HAPPIER WHEN THEY DO.

COME HOME!

I HOPE THERE'S NO PLAGUE COMING. THE SWINEHERD'S WIFE DIED A WEEK AGO, AND SHE THOUGHT SOMETHING SEIZED HER THROAT IN BED.

PAPA SAYS SUCH HORRIBLE FANCIES CAN ACCOMPANY FEVER. SHE WAS QUITE WELL THE DAY BEFORE.

WELL, *HER* FUNERAL IS OVER. WE SHAN'T BE TORTURED WITH MORE DISCORD AND JARGON. IT MAKES ME NERVOUS.

That evening, Father told us of another case similar to the two recent fatal ones. A peasant's sister had been attacked in the same way, and was now steadily sinking.

THESE POOR PEOPLE INFECT ONE ANOTHER WITH THEIR SUPERSTITIONS! ALL THIS IS NATURAL CAUSES.

BUT IT FRIGHTENS ONE HORRIBLY.

Later there arrived the son of the picture cleaner with our many portraits, which had undergone the process of restoration.

My mother was of an old Hungarian family, and most of these pictures came to us through her.

CARMILLA! YOU ARE *LIVING* IN THIS PICTURE!

THE NAME READS "MIRCALLA, COUNTESS KARNSTEIN, 1698." I AM DESCENDED FROM THE KARNSTEINS—THAT IS, MAMMA WAS.

AH! I AM ALSO OF VERY ANCIENT DESCENT. ARE THERE ANY KARNSTEINS LIVING NOW?

NO, BUT THE RUINS OF THE CASTLE ARE THREE MILES AWAY.

I SHOULD LIKE TO VISIT THEM. BUT SEE, WHAT BEAUTIFUL MOONLIGHT!

IT IS SO LIKE THE NIGHT YOU CAME TO US.

YOU DON'T KNOW HOW **DEAR** YOU ARE TO ME, BUT I DARE NOT TELL MY STORY YET, EVEN TO YOU. THE TIME IS NEAR WHEN YOU SHALL KNOW **EVERYTHING!**

YOU WILL THINK ME CRUEL, BUT LOVE IS SELFISH AND WILL HAVE ITS SACRIFICES.

NO SACRIFICE WITHOUT **BLOOD!**

BUT LET US GO TO SLEEP NOW.

I went to my room with an uncomfortable sensation.

I had adopted Carmilla's habit of locking her bedroom door, alarmed about midnight invaders.

Thus fortified, I might take my rest in peace. But dreams come through stone walls, laughing at locksmiths.

I had a dream I cannot call a nightmare, for I was quite conscious of being asleep...

I fancied something moving around the foot of the bed:

a sooty-black animal resembling a monstrous cat about five feet long.

Although terrified, I could not cry out...

It sprang lightly onto the bed. Suddenly I felt a stinging pain as if two large needles darted deep into my breast...

I woke with a scream...

...and saw a female figure standing there.

As I stared, it appeared to change place. Then the door opened, and it passed out.

I THINK CARMILLA HAS BEEN PLAYING A TRICK—BUT MY DOOR IS LOCKED ON THE INSIDE, AS USUAL!

I was afraid to open it; horrified. So I sprang back into bed.

21

I should have told papa, but I thought he might fancy that I had been attacked by the mysterious complaint which had invaded our neighborhood.

I HAD A FRIGHTENING DREAM LAST NIGHT AND I AWOKE AND THOUGHT I SAW A DARK FIGURE, BUT THEN IT DISAPPEARED.

I'M SURE IT WAS ALL FANCY. I USED TO THINK EVIL SPIRITS MADE DREAMS, BUT OUR DOCTOR TOLD ME IT'S ONLY A FEVER OR SOME MALADY.

Some nights I slept profoundly, but every morning I felt a languor that weighed on me all day. A strange melancholy, and thoughts of death took possession of me.

Strange sensations visited me in my sleep, as if a hand was drawn along my cheek and neck.

As if warm lips kissed me.

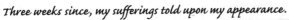

Three weeks since, my sufferings told upon my appearance.

YOU'VE GROWN PALE AND YOUR EYES ARE DILATED AND DARKENED UNDERNEATH. ARE YOU ILL?

I AM QUITE ...WELL.

In a sense, this was true. I had no pain. My complaint seemed to be one of the imagination or nerves.

One night, I thought I heard the voice of my mother, sweet and tender, yet terrible.

YOU MUST BEWARE OF THE ASSASSIN!

MAMA?

I looked for her, but instead saw Carmilla, bathed from her chin to her feet, in one great stain of blood!

I woke with a shriek, possessed with the idea Carmilla was being murdered.

HELP! HELP!

CARMILLA! CARMILLA!

Our calls were unanswered. All was vain.

FORCE THE LOCK.

CRACK!

We stared into the room...

...everything was undisturbed. But Carmilla was gone!

THE WINDOWS ARE SECURED!

EVERY PART OF THE CASTLE MUST BE SEARCHED!

The grounds were explored. No trace of the missing lady could be discovered.

It was after noon when I went up to her room. I was astounded to find her standing calmly at her dressing table!

GASP!

DEAR CARMILLA!

WHERE HAVE YOU **BEEN** ALL THIS TIME?

LAST NIGHT HAS BEEN A NIGHT OF WONDERS.

MERCY'S SAKE, EXPLAIN!

I WENT TO SLEEP IN MY BED AS USUAL, BUT I WOKE JUST NOW ON THE SOFA, AND FOUND THE DOOR HAD BEEN FORCED.

HOW COULD THIS HAVE HAPPENED WITHOUT MY BEING WAKENED?

MAY I ASK YOU A QUESTION?

I'LL TELL YOU EVERYTHING, BUT MY STORY IS OF BEWILDERMENT AND DARKNESS.

HAVE YOU EVER BEEN SUSPECTED OF SLEEPWALKING?

NOT SINCE I WAS VERY YOUNG.

YOU GOT UP IN YOUR SLEEP, UNLOCKED THE DOOR AND RELOCKED IT ON THE OUTSIDE.

PAPA, HOW DO YOU ACCOUNT FOR HER FINDING HERSELF ON THE SOFA, WHICH WE HAD SEARCHED CAREFULLY?

SHE CAME AFTER YOU SEARCHED, STILL ASLEEP, AND AWOKE SPONTANEOUSLY...

I WISH **ALL** MYSTERIES WERE AS EASILY EXPLAINED.

Father arranged that a servant should sleep outside her door, so she could not make another such excursion.

The next morning, my father called me to the library.

LAURA, DEAR, COME ATTEND TO DR. SPIELSBERG FOR A MOMENT...

YOU MENTIONED A SENSATION LIKE TWO NEEDLES PIERCING YOUR NECK WHEN YOU EXPERIENCED YOUR FIRST HORRIBLE DREAM. IS THERE STILL ANY SORENESS?

NONE AT ALL.

IT WAS HERE, BELOW MY THROAT.

GOD FORBID!

YOU SEE IT NOW WITH YOUR OWN EYES!

WHAT *IS* IT?

NOTHING BUT A SMALL BLUE SPOT, MY DEAR.

THE QUESTION IS, WHAT NOW IS BEST TO BE DONE?

WHAT *CAN* BE DONE?

I ADVISE A CONSULTATION WITH BARON VORDENBURG IN GRATZ. HE IS THE ONLY KNOWN EXPERT IN SUCH MATTERS.

MEANWHILE, SEEK THE ASSISTANCE OF THE PRIEST IN KARNSTEIN.

AND YOU MUST NOT LET LAURA ALONE FOR ONE MOMENT. THAT IS INDISPENSABLE.

I WILL SEE TO IT.

Father, Madame and I made a visit to Karnstein to see the priest.

Turning a curve, we encountered our old friend, the General, riding toward us.

GENERAL SPIELSDORF!

He accepted the vacant seat in our carriage. In the ten months since we had seen him, he had grown thinner. Gloom and anxiety had taken the place of cordial serenity.

Father looked at him with alarm. I could see he feared for the General's sanity.

THE YEARS REMAINING TO ME ON EARTH MAY NOT BE LONG, BUT I HOPE TO DELIVER THE **VENGEANCE OF HEAVEN** UPON THE FIENDS WHO MURDERED MY NIECE!

WE HAD AN INVITATION FROM MY OLD FRIEND, COUNT CARLSFELD, ON THE OTHER SIDE OF KARNSTEIN, TO ATTEND A FÊTE IN HONOR OF THE GRAND DUKE CHARLES. THE NIGHT WAS A MAGNIFICENT MASQUERADE...

I NOTICED A YOUNG LADY WHO APPEARED TO BE OBSERVING MY WARD WITH EXTRAORDINARY INTEREST. A LADY WITH A STATELY AIR ACCOMPANIED HER AS A CHAPERON.

MY DEAR CHILD WAS RESTING IN A CHAIR WHEN THEY APPROACHED. THE YOUNGER ONE TOOK THE CHAIR NEXT TO MY WARD.

AFTER A TIME THEY HAD GROWN VERY GOOD FRIENDS, AND THE STRANGER — WHOM HER MOTHER CALLED MILLARCA — LOWERED HER MASK, DISPLAYING A REMARKABLY BEAUTIFUL FACE.

MY POOR CHILD HAS NOT QUITE RECOVERED HER STRENGTH. HER HORSE FELL WITH HER, AND OUR PHYSICIAN SAYS SHE MUST ON NO ACCOUNT EXERT HERSELF FOR SOME TIME TO COME.

I HESITATE TO ASK, BUT COULD YOU POSSIBLY TAKE CHARGE OF HER DURING MY ABSENCE?

THIS WAS AN AUDACIOUS REQUEST, BUT I HAD NOT A MOMENT TO THINK ABOUT IT.

THERE IS SOMETHING EXTREMELY ENGAGING ABOUT HER FACE, AS WELL AS THE ELEGANCE AND FIRE OF HIGH BIRTH.

PLEASE INVITE MY FRIEND TO STAY WITH US!

QUITE OVERPOWERED, I SUBMITTED.

NO ATTEMPT IS TO BE MADE TO LEARN MORE ABOUT HER UNTIL MY RETURN.

I COMMIT MYSELF ENTIRELY TO YOUR HONOR.

THE BALL WAS NOT OVER UNTIL THE MORNING SUN, WHEN MY WARD ASKED ME...

WHAT HAS BECOME OF MILLARCA?

I THOUGHT SHE WAS BY YOUR SIDE!

I FANCIED SHE WAS BY *YOURS!*

ALL EFFORTS TO FIND HER WERE IN VAIN.

I NOW RECOGNIZE THE FOLLY IN HAVING UNDERTAKEN CHARGE OF A YOUNG LADY WITHOUT SO MUCH AS KNOWING HER NAME!

IT WAS NOT 'TIL TWO THE NEXT AFTERNOON THAT WE HEARD ANYTHING, WHEN A SERVANT KNOCKED AT OUR DOOR.

I'VE BEEN REQUESTED BY A YOUNG LADY IN GREAT DISTRESS TO FIND GENERAL SPIELSDORF AND HIS DAUGHTER.

SHE TOLD A STORY TO ACCOUNT FOR HER DISAPPEARANCE.

I GOT TO THE HOUSEKEEPER'S BEDROOM IN DESPAIR OF FINDING YOU, AND FELL INTO A DEEP SLEEP.

THAT DAY MILLARCA CAME HOME WITH US. I WAS ONLY TOO HAPPY TO HAVE SECURED A CHARMING COMPANION FOR MY GIRL.

THERE SOON, HOWEVER, APPEARED SOME DRAWBACKS.

SHE COMPLAINED OF EXTREME LANGUOR AND NEVER EMERGED FROM HER ROOM 'TIL THE AFTERNOON.

AND ALTHOUGH SHE ALWAYS LOCKED HER DOOR ON THE INSIDE, SHE WAS SOMETIMES ABSENT FROM HER ROOM IN THE MORNING.

SHE WAS REPEATEDLY SEEN IN THE MORNING, WALKING THROUGH THE TREES, LOOKING AS IF IN A TRANCE.

THIS CONVINCED ME SHE WALKED IN HER SLEEP.

BUT HOW DID SHE PASS FROM HER ROOM, WITHOUT UNBARRING DOOR OR WINDOW? IN THE MIDST OF MY PERPLEXITIES, AN ANXIETY FAR MORE URGENT PRESENTED ITSELF...

MY DEAR CHILD BEGAN TO LOSE HER HEALTH, IN A MANNER SO MYSTERIOUS I BECAME FRIGHTENED. SHE WAS VISITED BY APPALLING DREAMS AND FANCIED A SPECTRE WALKING 'ROUND THE FOOT OF HER BED.

SHE FELT SOMETHING LIKE LARGE NEEDLES PIERCE HER, A LITTLE BELOW THE THROAT, FOLLOWED BY A GRADUAL SENSE OF STRANGULATION AND UNCONSCIOUSNESS.

STRANGE! THOSE ARE MY OWN SYMPTOMS EXACTLY DESCRIBED! AND HE'S DETAILING THE PECULIARITIES OF CARMILLA!

A vista opened in the forest, and we halted at the ruined village.

We entered the crumbling castle.

THIS WAS ONCE THE PALATIAL RESIDENCE OF THE KARNSTEINS — A BAD FAMILY, AND HERE ITS BLOODSTAINED ANNALS WERE WRITTEN!

AND SOMEWHERE NEAR THAT CHAPEL IS WHAT I SEEK: THE HIDDEN GRAVE OF MIRCALLA, COUNTESS OF KARNSTEIN!

WE HAVE A PORTRAIT OF THE COUNTESS AT HOME; SHOULD YOU LIKE TO SEE IT?

I'VE SEEN THE ORIGINAL.

BUT SHE'S BEEN *DEAD* MORE THAN A *CENTURY!*

NOT SO DEAD AS YOU FANCY.

GENERAL, YOU PUZZLE ME.

THERE REMAINS BUT ONE OBJECT WHICH CAN INTEREST ME: TO WREAK ON HER THE VENGEANCE WHICH MAY STILL BE ACCOMPLISHED BY A MORTAL ARM!

WHAT VENGEANCE CAN YOU MEAN?

I MEAN TO *DECAPITATE* THE MONSTER!

WHAT?

The General continued his story...

MY BELOVED CHILD WAS GROWING WORSE. RATHER THAN TRY NOTHING, I CONCEALED MYSELF IN HER DRESSING ROOM AND WATCHED 'TIL SHE WAS FAST ASLEEP.

THEN I SAW A BLACK SHAPE, VERY ILL-DEFINED, CRAWL OVER THE BED AND UP TO HER THROAT, WHERE IT SWELLED INTO A GREAT, PALPITATING MASS.

I STOOD PETRIFIED.

I NOW SPRANG FORWARD. THE CREATURE CONTRACTED AND, STANDING ON THE FLOOR, WITH A GLARE OF SKULKING FEROCITY AND HORROR FIXED ON ME....

....I SAW MILLARCA!

I STRUCK AT HER INSTANTLY WITH MY SWORD, BUT SHE WAS GONE.

I ORDERED A SEARCH, BUT MILLARCA WAS GONE. HER VICTIM WAS SINKING FAST, AND BEFORE MORNING DAWNED, SHE DIED.

The old General leaned against the wall and sighed.
I then saw Carmilla enter the shadowy chapel.

Before I could scream, he struck at her with all his force, but she dived under his blow...

WHERE IS CARMILLA? WHERE IS CARMILLA?

...and was gone!

I DON'T KNOW.... SHE WENT *THERE.*

CARMILLA! CARMILLA!

SHE CALLED HERSELF *CARMILLA?*

THAT IS *MILLARCA,* AND ALSO *MIRCALLA,* COUNTESS OF KARNSTEIN!

DEPART FROM THIS ACCURSED GROUND, QUICKLY! AND MAY YOU *NEVER AGAIN* BEHOLD CARMILLA!

Waiting for us at home was Baron Vordenburg, one of the strangest-looking men I ever beheld.

DOCTOR SPIELSBERG TOLD ME OF YOUR TROUBLES. MY FAMILY HAS A RATHER.... UNFORTUNATE ASSOCIATION WITH THE KARNSTEINS.

IN HIS YOUTH, MY ANCESTOR HAD BEEN A LOVER OF MIRCALLA. HER EARLY DEATH *BY HER OWN HAND* PLUNGED HIM INTO INCONSOLABLE GRIEF.

SOME TIME LATER, THE REGION BEGAN TO BE TROUBLED BY REVENANTS, A HORROR WHICH CONTINUES TODAY.

YOU HAVE HEARD RUMORS OF THE VAMPIRE, WHICH I FIND LARGELY FACTUAL.

40

A *SUICIDE* BECOMES A *VAMPIRE*. THAT SPECTRE VISITS PEOPLE IN THEIR SLUMBERS; **THEY** DIE AND DEVELOP INTO VAMPIRES. THAT IS HOW IT MULTIPLIES. THIS HAPPENED IN THE CASE OF MIRCALLA.

MY ANCESTOR RESOLVED TO SAVE MIRCALLA FROM DISCOVERY BY THE OBLITERATION OF HER MONUMENT. IT HAS SINCE BEEN FORGOTTEN.

THEN I AM *FOILED!*

NOT NECESSARILY.

I'VE TAKEN UP THE STUDY OF THIS PHENOMENON. THE CREATURES CAN ONLY BE DEFEATED BY TRACKING THEM TO THEIR GRAVES. THERE THEY MUST BE EXTINGUISHED BY THE STAKE, BY DECAPITATION, AND BY BURNING.

WHEN AGE HAD STOLEN UPON MY ANCESTOR, HE LOOKED BACK WITH REGRET ON WHAT HE HAD DONE. HE MADE NOTES WHICH REVEALED THE LOCATION OF THE GRAVE OF MIRCALLA.

THESE PAPERS WERE PASSED ON TO ME, AND IT MAY NOW BE FOR US TO FINALLY BRING AN END TO THE TERROR!

THEN THE HORRIBLE ENEMY MAY *YET* BE DEFEATED! FIRST THING TOMORROW, WE RETURN TO KARNSTEIN!

The next day we returned to the ruined chapel.

RIP
MIRCALLA
COUNTESS
KARNSTEIN

Though a hundred and fifty years had passed since her funeral, her features were tinted with the warmth of life, and the leaden coffin floated with blood!

I swooned and awoke outside the chapel. The territory has never since been plagued by the visits of a vampire.

Ten years later, I now write all this, you suppose, with composure. But far from it; I cannot think of it without agitation.

It was long before the terror of the events subsided, and to this hour the image of Carmilla returns to memory—sometimes the languid, beautiful girl—sometimes the writhing fiend I saw in the ruined church; and often from a reverie I have started, fancying I heard the light step of Carmilla at the drawing room door.

ILLUSTRATONS ©2007 LISA K. WEBER

The Mysteries of Udolpho

by Ann Radcliffe

script by **Antonella Caputo**
illustrated by **Carlo Vergara**

Emily stood gazing from the window of her chamber in the castle of Udolpho. The night air refreshed her as she looked on the shadowy scene, over which the planets silently moved in their destined course.

She remembered how often she had gazed on them with her dear father. The stars brought a retrospect of all the strange events which had occurred since she lived in peace with her dear parents.

Was it only a year ago – her sixteenth summer – that she lived with her family in the modest ancestral château of her father, Monsieur St. Aubert?

Her favorite walk was to the little fishing house belonging to her father.

She recalled the day that she observed some lines written with a pencil on a part of the wainscot.

*Go, pencil! faithful to thy master's sighs!
Go — tell the Goddess of the fairy scene,
When next her light steps wind these wood-walks green,
Whence all his tears, his tender sorrows, rise;
And who that gazes on that angel-smile,
Would fear its charm, or think it could beguile!*

Often she had wondered about the identity of the author, and she suspected herself as the subject.

But soon the tranquility of her life was shattered. Madame St. Aubert was attacked with a fever. On the seventh day she succumbed to her disease.

His wife had hardly been interred when Monsieur St. Aubert began to display the same symptoms.

The physician had prescribed the air of Languedoc and Provence.

Despite her concerns for her father's health, Emily could not restrain her delight in the pine forests of the mountains.

As they crossed the Pyrenees, St. Aubert looked from the carriage and saw a young man step from the bushes.

The stranger, whose name was Valancourt, proposed to travel on with them.

St. Aubert invited him to accompany them for a few days since he found that he was of a family with which he was well-acquainted. The latter accepted the offer with pleasure.

St. Aubert found great pleasure in conversing with Valancourt…

…and Valancourt was so charmed with his companions that he seemed to have forgotten he had any further to go.

It was St. Aubert's plan to proceed to the border of the Mediterranean and travel along its shore. Valancourt reluctantly left them.

For a brief time the fresh air and the scenery had revived St. Aubert, but soon the strains of traveling became too much for him, and they sought refuge in the convent of St. Claire.

In his final hours, St. Aubert had appointed his sister, Madame Cheron, as Emily's guardian.

He was interred in the churchyard of the convent.

Emily, after her return to La Vallée, received letters from her aunt in which she announced her plans to come and escort Emily to Toulouse, and added that, as her brother had entrusted Emily's *education* to her, she should consider herself bound to overlook her *conduct*.

Several weeks passed in quiet retirement. Then one day she saw Valancourt coming towards the château.

I HAVE TAKEN A COMMISSION, AND MUST JOIN MY REGIMENT IN PARIS. LET ME VENTURE TO DECLARE THE ADMIRATION I MUST ALWAYS FEEL OF YOUR GOODNESS.

OH! THAT AT SOME FUTURE PERIOD I MIGHT BE PERMITTED TO CALL IT *LOVE*!

Emily's reply was cut short by the arrival of Madame Cheron.

SO NIECE, HOW DO YOU DO? BUT I NEED NOT ASK; YOUR LOOKS TELL ME YOU HAVE ALREADY RECOVERED YOUR LOSS!

MY LOOKS DO ME INJUSTICE, MADAME. MY LOSS CAN *NEVER* BE RECOVERED.

...MAY I INTRODUCE YOU TO CHEVALIER VALANCOURT.

I SEE...!

Valancourt took his leave of Emily in a manner that expressed his pain at his own departure, and at leaving her with Madame Cheron.

WHO *IS* THAT YOUNG MAN? I CAN PERCEIVE THAT YOU IMAGINE YOURSELF TO BE VIOLENTLY IN *LOVE* WITH HIM.

Madame Cheron had been some years a widow and resided on her own estate near Toulouse. Emily found her to be a vain and bitter woman. Yet she remembered her father's final words...

SHE IS NOT EXACTLY THE PERSON TO WHOM I WOULD HAVE COMMITTED YOU...

...BUT SHE IS YOUR ONLY FEMALE RELATION. I NEED NOT RECOMMEND IT TO YOUR PRUDENCE, MY LOVE, TO ENDEAVOR TO CONCILIATE HER KINDNESS.

Madame Charon entertained frequently.

At first Emily was struck by the apparent knowledge displayed by the guests.

At length, she perceived that the animation exhibited by them resulted mostly from a desire to draw attention to themselves.

One morning Emily was summoned and Madame Cheron held out a letter.

I WILL **NOT** BE DISTURBED IN MY OWN HOUSE BY ANY LETTERS FROM YOUNG MEN!

IF YOU ARE NOT CONTENT TO CONFORM TO MY DIRECTION I SHALL SEND YOU TO BOARD IN A CONVENT!

That afternoon, as Emily sat in the garden, Valancourt arrived.

HAVE YOU SPOKEN TO MADAME CHERON?

NO, I HAVE NOT YET SEEN HER.

Madame Cheron had a private conversation with Valancourt. When she returned to the château, her countenance expressed ill humor.

I HAVE DISMISSED THIS YOUNG MAN, AT LAST. HE HAD THE **PRESUMPTION** TO SUPPOSE I WOULD MARRY MY NIECE TO A PERSON SUCH AS HE DESCRIBES HIMSELF! IF YOU CONCERT ANY MEANS OF INTERVIEW UNKNOWN TO ME, YOU SHALL LEAVE MY HOUSE **IMMEDIATELY!**

Among the frequent visitors of Madame Cheron were two Italian gentlemen: Signor Montoni, who had an air of conscious superiority, and Signor Cavigni, inferior in dignity, but superior in insinuation of manner.

Montoni soon became a daily guest at the Château, and Emily was compelled to observe that he was a suitor to her aunt.

Madame Cheron's avarice conspired with her vanity, as she fancied herself the wife of an Italian count.

One morning, Emily was summoned to attend Madame Cheron.

SO, NIECE, I HAVE NEWS TO TELL YOU.

FROM THIS HOUR YOU MUST CONSIDER SIGNOR MONTONI AS YOUR UNCLE — WE WERE MARRIED THIS MORNING!

Montoni now took possession of the château and the command of its inhabitants with the ease of a man who had long considered it to be his own.

Within few days Madame Montoni gave a magnificent entertainment. She danced, laughed and talked incessantly, while Montoni, silent and reserved, seemed weary of the frivolous company.

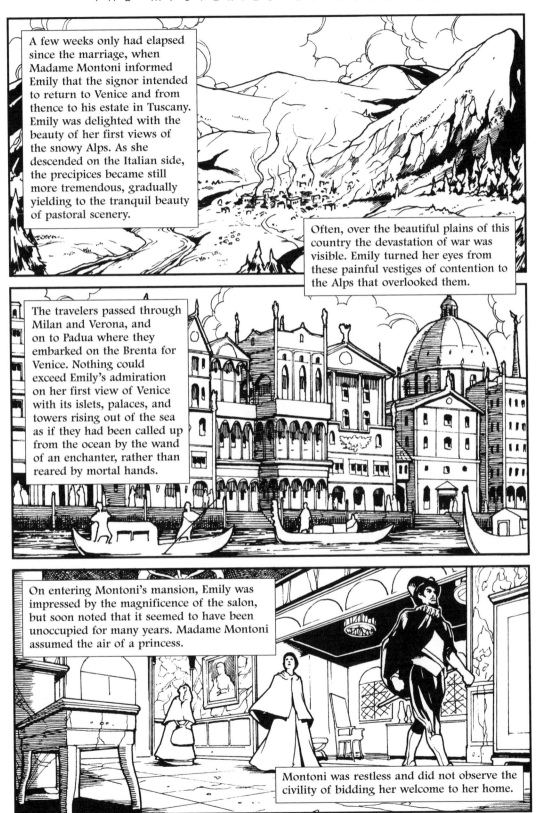

A few weeks only had elapsed since the marriage, when Madame Montoni informed Emily that the signor intended to return to Venice and from thence to his estate in Tuscany. Emily was delighted with the beauty of her first views of the snowy Alps. As she descended on the Italian side, the precipices became still more tremendous, gradually yielding to the tranquil beauty of pastoral scenery.

Often, over the beautiful plains of this country the devastation of war was visible. Emily turned her eyes from these painful vestiges of contention to the Alps that overlooked them.

The travelers passed through Milan and Verona, and on to Padua where they embarked on the Brenta for Venice. Nothing could exceed Emily's admiration on her first view of Venice with its islets, palaces, and towers rising out of the sea as if they had been called up from the ocean by the wand of an enchanter, rather than reared by mortal hands.

On entering Montoni's mansion, Emily was impressed by the magnificence of the salon, but soon noted that it seemed to have been unoccupied for many years. Madame Montoni assumed the air of a princess.

Montoni was restless and did not observe the civility of bidding her welcome to her home.

Over the years Montoni had lost heavily at the gaming tables and now stood on the brink of financial ruin.

He passed the night with a party of young men who had more money than rank, and more vice than either.

Such were the friends whom Montoni introduced to his family on the day after his arrival at Venice.

Several weeks passed, as Emily took interest in the scenes that surrounded her.

I HAVE BEEN THINKING I SHOULD COLLECT THE RENT AT UDOLPHO. WE CAN SPEND A COUPLE OF WEEKS THERE.

THE CASTLE OF UDOLPHO!

Emily listened to the mention of this journey with anticipation.

Montoni, who had been allured by the seeming wealth of Madame Cheron, was now disappointed by her holdings.

Madame Montoni had contrived to have the greatest part of what she really did possess settled upon herself.

Then came the morning that Emily was awakened by a quick knocking at her door.

ANNETTE, WHAT BRINGS YOU HITHER SO EARLY?

I ONLY KNOW THAT THE SIGNOR HAS HAD US ALL CALLED OUT OF OUR BEDS AND TELLS US WE ARE ALL TO LEAVE VENICE IMMEDIATELY.

I HEAR THE OARS ON THE CANAL: IT'S THE GONDOLA!

Emily prepared for this unexpected flight, believing that any change in her position could not be for the worse.

Montoni refused all questions while Emily's aunt appeared to be as ignorant as herself and to undertake the journey with some reluctance.

Politics and debt had twined about Montoni to the point that he considered it imperative that he relocate to his castle with all haste.

Montoni pursued his way by carriage across the country towards the Apennines. Steep rose over steep; the mountains seemed to multiply as they went and what was the summit of one eminence proved to be only the base of another.

The travelers continued to ascend until they entered a narrow pass, which opened to a mountain scene as wild as any they had yet passed.

"There," said Montoni, speaking for the first time in several hours, "is Udolpho."

As the carriage wheels rolled under the portcullis, Emily's heart sank and it seemed to her as if she was going into a prison.

SKREEECKK.... SKREECCKK.

She entered an extensive gothic hall. From the contemplation of this scene the remembrance of Valancourt, far, far distant, came to her heart and softened into sorrow.

MAY I ASK, SIR, THE MOTIVE OF THIS SUDDEN JOURNEY?

IT DOES NOT SUIT ME TO ANSWER INQUIRIES. I RECOMMEND IT TO YOU TO RETIRE TO YOUR CHAMBER.

ANNETTE!

MY LADY'S ROOM IS AT THE OTHER END OF THE CASTLE.

WHAT A WILD PLACE THIS IS, MA'AM!

PLEASE! DO NOT GO IN THERE!

WHY DO YOU HESITATE? LET ME SEE WHITHER THIS ROOM LEADS!

DO LET US GO... THIS IS SURELY WHAT THEY TOLD ME OF IN VENICE!

I WISH TO EXAMINE THE PICTURE. TAKE THE LIGHT, WHILE I LIFT THE VEIL.

DID YOU EVER HEAR OF THE STRANGE ACCIDENT THAT MADE THE SIGNOR LORD OF THIS CASTLE? BY SOME LAW OR OTHER IT WAS TO COME TO THE SIGNOR IF THE LADY DIED UNMARRIED.

WHAT LADY?

THIS HAPPENED MANY YEARS AGO WHEN SIGNOR MONTONI WAS YOUNG.

THE LADY, SIGNORA LAURENTINI, WAS VERY HANDSOME. IT WAS ONE EVENING AT THE LATTER PART OF THE YEAR THIS GRAND LADY WALKED OUT OF THE CASTLE INTO THE WOOD BELOW...

THE SERVANTS SEARCHED ALL NIGHT LONG. BUT COULD NOT FIND ANY TRACE OF HER!

Emily struggled to overcome her fear and dismissed Annette for the night.

Daylight dispelled from Emily's mind the gloom of superstition, but not the apprehension. She endeavored to amuse herself by a view of the gothic magnificence of Udolpho. This brought to her recollection the veiled picture.

Having paused a moment at the door, Emily hastily entered the chamber.

Then, with a timid hand, she lifted the veil...

...but instantly let it fall!

She dropped senseless to the floor.

Emily remained for many weeks confined within the walls of Udolpho.

Her only friends were Annette and her consort Ludovico, a servant of Signor Cavigni.

One night Emily perceived the faint sweet note of a lute. She tried to ascertain from what quarter the sounds proceeded, but they soon halted.

IF THOSE SOUNDS WERE *HUMAN*, I SHALL PROBABLY HEAR THEM AGAIN!

Early the following morning Emily heard a noisy bustle in the courtyard. She knew that there was much fighting among the small states of Italy, and they often employed bands of mercenary soldiers.

Emily reasoned that Montoni was the captain of such a band of condottieri, and that this castle had become a place of rendezvous.

She went to Madame Montoni and mentioned what had occurred; but her aunt could not give any explanation. Then Montoni himself appeared.

I INSIST UPON KNOWING THIS INSTANT WHAT ALL THIS MEANS!

OTHER BUSINESS BROUGHT ME HERE. THOSE ESTATES OF YOURS MUST BE GIVEN UP, WITHOUT FURTHER CONTENTION!

WHAT IS THE REASON FOR THESE ARMED MEN? AM I TO BE SHUT UP HERE, TO BE KILLED?

THAT MAY *HAPPEN* UNLESS YOU YIELD TO MY DEMAND. YOU SHALL BE *REMOVED* TO THE EAST TURRET. YOU MAY UNDERSTAND THE DANGER OF OFFENDING A MAN WHO HAS AN *UNLIMITED POWER* OVER YOU...!

MEN, EXECUTE YOUR ORDERS!

AAAAAAAAAAHH!

When Emily recovered, she was alone. She stepped timidly out into the gallery and made her way back to her own chamber.

Emily remained in her chamber until the following morning. She determined to go to Montoni and to entreat that he would suffer her to see Madame Montoni. She begged him to tell her where her aunt was.

SHE *SUFFERS* BY HER OWN *FOLLY!* LET HER BE OBEDIENT AND SIGN THE WRITINGS AND I WILL THINK NO MORE OF IT!

The hours passed in solitude. It appeared that Montoni had wholly forgotten her. Emily recollected the mysterious strain of music she had heard, and determined to watch alone at her window. She was soon recalled from the reverie into which she had sunk by a sound like the mourning of some person in distress.

She thought she saw something moving and she then distinguished a human form. Suddenly, the figure darted away and was lost in the obscurity of the night.

Several days later, Emily inquired of Annette whether any person in the castle played a musical instrument.

OH YES, BENEDETTO PLAYS THE DRUM, AND THERE IS LAUNCELOT, THE TRUMPETER...

HAVE YOU HEARD NO OTHER MUSIC IN THE CASTLE – LATE AT NIGHT?

...AS FOR LAST NIGHT, I DID NOTHING BUT DREAM I SAW MY LATE LADY'S GHOST...

YOUR *LATE* LADY'S!

YOU HAVE HEARD SOMETHING THEN!

NAY, MA'MSELLE. NOBODY KNOWS *ANYTHING* OF HER!

IT IS PLAIN, THEREFORE, THAT SHE IS GONE!

The remarks of Annette revived Emily's terrible suspicions concerning the fate of Madame Montoni.

When night returned, she resumed her station at the casement. It was very late when her ear suddenly caught the notes of distant music. She recognized one of the popular airs of her native province! Could the mysterious prisoner possibly be Valancourt?

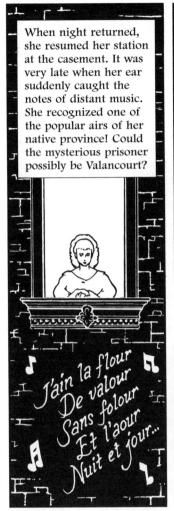

*J'ain la flour
De valour
Sans folour
Et l'aour
Nuit et jour...*

In the morning, Emily enquired of Annette if she had heard talk of prisoners.

I DO BELIEVE THERE ARE PRISONERS, FOR I OVERHEARD ONE OF THE SIGNOR'S MEN SAYING WHAT A FINE THING IT WAS TO CATCH UP MEN, BECAUSE OF THE RANSOM.

It had been almost a week since Emily had seen Madame Montoni, and she now held little hope that she still lived.

I – I WISH TO RETURN TO FRANCE. NOW THAT MY AUNT IS NO MORE, I SHOULD BE PERMITTED TO DEPART.

WHO *TOLD* YOU THAT MADAME MONTONI WAS DEAD?

IF YOU WISH TO SEE HER, SHE LIES IN THE EAST TURRET.

Emily made her way to the turret, and slowly opened the door unto a dusky and silent chamber, when a hollow voice spoke!

E – EMILY!

DO YOU INDEED *LIVE* OR IS THIS BUT A TERRIBLE *APPARITION?*

I THOUGHT YOU HAD FORSAKEN ME. I DO LIVE, BUT – I FEEL THAT I AM ABOUT TO DIE!

Emily, after a time, left her aunt's side and sought out Montoni.

MADAME MONTONI IS *DYING*, SIR! SUFFER HER TO BE REMOVED FROM THAT FORLORN ROOM TO HER OWN APARTMENT AND TO HAVE NECESSARY COMFORT ADMINISTERED!

OF WHAT SERVICE WILL *THAT* BE, IF SHE IS DYING?

Finally he consented that his wife should be removed to her own apartments and that Emily should attend her.

WILL YOU NOW SIGN OVER THE ESTATES?

YOU SHALL *NEVER* HAVE THEM...

At length she revived and directed Emily where to find the papers relative to her estates in France.

After midnight she was gone forever.

When Montoni found that his wife had died without giving him the necessary signature, no sense of decency restrained his resentment.

THUD!

Several days passed, then Montoni requested a meeting with Emily.

I SENT FOR YOU THAT YOU MIGHT BE A WITNESS IN SOME BUSINESS WHICH I AM TRANSACTING.

ALL THAT IS REQUIRED OF YOU WILL BE TO SIGN YOUR NAME TO THIS PAPER.

I–I DO NOT WISH TO SIGN IT.

I AM THE HEIR OF *ALL* MADAME MONTONI POSSESSED! THAT WHICH SHE REFUSED TO ME IN HER LIFETIME CAN NO *LONGER* BE WITHHELD!

I AM *NOT* SO IGNORANT! THE LAW GIVES ME THE ESTATES IN QUESTION, AND MY OWN HAND SHALL *NEVER* BETRAY MY RIGHTS!

YOU *SPEAK* LIKE A HEROINE...

WE SHALL SEE WHETHER YOU CAN *SUFFER* LIKE ONE!

Emily went to her aunt's former apartment and there found the concealed papers relative to the estates. As she examined the papers, a peal of laughter rose from the terrace.

TELL ME ANNETTE, WHO ARE THOSE PERSONS?

HA! HA! HA!...

THEY ARE JUST COME. THEY MUST SURELY BE **MAD** TO COME FREELY TO SUCH A PLACE AS THIS!

OH, MA'AMSELLE, IF I COULD BUT CATCH THE GREAT GATE OPEN FOR ONE MINUTE, IT SHOULD NEVER SEE ME AGAIN!

IT MAY, PERHAPS, BE IN **LUDOVICO'S** POWER, TO EFFECT OUR ESCAPE. GO TO HIM, ANNETTE, BUT ENTREAT HIM TO BE SECRET. IF HE IS WILLING TO UNDERTAKE THIS HE SHALL BE AMPLY REWARDED!

AND PLEASE ASK HIM IF HE HAS ANY KNOWLEDGE OF **PRISONERS** IN THE CASTLE.

In that evening, as Emily walked for air in the gallery adjoining her chamber, she found herself clasped in a man's strong arms!

HA! I HAVE YOU AT LAST..!

MY CHARMING EMILY, RETURN WITH ME TO THE PARTY!

FOR HEAVEN'S SAKE, LET ME GO!

She recognized the man as Verezzi, one of Montoni's officers.

With a desperate effort she managed to liberate herself and she fled to her chamber. It appeared to her that Montoni had commenced his scheme of vengeance. She knew that Montoni had lost a large sum to Verezzi, so there was the terrible possibility of his designing her to be a substitute for the debt!

Several days passed. Ludovico could only learn that there was a prisoner and he was Frenchman.

THERE IS NO OTHER PLACE IN THE CASTLE, BESIDES THIS CORRIDOR, WHERE YOU CAN SEE HIM IN SAFETY.

THE CHEVALIER WOULD NOT ENTRUST ME WITH HIS NAME, BUT WHEN I MENTIONED YOURS, HE SEEMED OVERWHELMED WITH JOY. I MAY BE ABLE TO ARRANGE A MEETING WITH YOU.

Emily's impatience increased with her fear. It became more probable that Valancourt was here a prisoner!

It was settled that the Chevalier should meet her in the corridor. Emily was much agitated by the near prospect of meeting Valancourt.

OH!

MY APOLOGIES, MADEMOISELLE. YOU ARE NO STRANGER TO ME. MY NAME IS DU PONT AND I HAVE LONG, LONG LOVED YOU...

MY FAMILY LIVED NEAR LA VALLÉE. I OFTEN VISITED YOUR FISHING-HOUSE, BUT CHIVALRY FORBADE ME TO REVEAL MY PASSION, EXCEPT IN A POEM I SCRIBED.

PLEASE ACCEPT THE OFFERED SERVICES OF A FRIEND.

Suddenly Verezzi leapt from the shadows!

I WILL OFFER YOU MY SERVICES!

The Chevalier quickly felled his attacker.

UNNHHH!

62

OTHERS WILL COME! FOLLOW ME, *QUICKLY!*

THE GATES WERE OPEN TO A PARTY JUST COME IN FROM THE MOUNTAINS.

THEY WILL BE SHUT, I FEAR, BEFORE WE CAN REACH THEM!

HUSH! IF YOU WILL REMAIN HERE I WILL GO TO SEE WHETHER THE GATES ARE OPEN.

WE HAVE NOT AN *INSTANT* TO LOSE!

I'LL WATCH THIS GATE, IF YOU WILL DO A GOOD TURN FOR ME AND GO AND FETCH THE WINE.

I WON'T KEEP YOU BUT A MINUTE!

TAKE YOUR TIME, I AM NOT IN HASTE.

They passed the dreadful gate and took the road that led down among the woods. Emily was so astonished by this sudden departure that she scarcely dared to believe herself awake.

It was determined they should descend into Tuscany where they could readily embark for France.

WHAT SHALL WE DO FOR MONEY? NEITHER OF US HAS A SINGLE SEQUIN!

La Tavern

The morning light showed a little town. There they there found a house which could afford shelter for themselves and the horses.

Du Pont ventured to inform the landlord of their situation, when suddenly Ludovico entered the room half frantic with joy.

On removing the saddle from one horse he had found beneath it a small bag containing more than sufficient money to carry them all to France.

The travelers exchanged their horses and recommenced their joyous way toward Livorno, which was the nearest port of consequence.

They traveled through the romantic mountain country and began to descend into the Valle of Arno. Emily took the opportunity of enquiring by what accident Du Pont had become Montoni's prisoner.

"I came into Italy in the service of my country. My regiment was camped near the castle of Udolpho, when I was told the identity of its master."

"I remembered that your aunt had married an Italian named Montoni, and that you had accompanied them into Italy..."

"I was coming to speak with you when I was captured by one of Montoni's raiding parties."

"My days in captivity were long and tedious. I frequently beguiled myself with an old lute, procured for me by a soldier."

"After some time one of my jailers gave me the means of walking on the terrace. In one of these midnight strolls I saw a light in a casement."

"It occurred to me that you might be in that apartment."

IT WAS YOU THEN, WHO OCCASIONED ME SUCH FOOLISH TERROR WHEN I SAW YOU IN THE SHADOW!

I REGRET HAVING CAUSED YOU ANY APPREHENSION!

Following several days' journey, the travelers arrived in Livorno. They immediately went down to the quay and booked passage on a ship for Marseilles and then towards Narbonne. Before returning to La Vallée, Emily wished to visit the convent of St. Claire, where her father was buried.

In Languedoc, on the shore of the Mediterranean, but a mile from Emily's destination, stood the Châteaule-le-Blanc.

It had been abandoned by the late Marquis. The Count De Villefort, who had succeeded to this estate, insisted that the family be reunited in the hereditary property of his ancestor.

The young Lady Blanche, who was not yet eighteen, had been confined to a convent, where she was placed immediately on her father's second marriage. Now she was free, and she was delighted with her new freedom.

She and her father, along with her brother Henri and her stepmother, the Countess, had occupied the property but a week before.

Blanche heard the faint report of guns. Her father, hearing the distress signal, joined her at the window. He sent his people out upon the cliff with torches, hoping they might prove a beacon to the vessel.

The count gave orders for his own boats to assist in bringing the crew of the vessel to shore, and that the unfortunate strangers should be brought to the château.

Among the passengers were Emily St. Aubert, Monsieur Du Pont, Ludovico and Annette.

They were graciously received by the Count and his family, who insisted that they stay in the château for the night.

In Monsieur Du Pont, the Count discovered the son of an old acquaintance.

The unaffected kindness of Blanche revived Emily's languid spirits.

Annette, meanwhile, was telling of the dangers they had encountered and congratulating herself so heartily upon her own escape that she made the château ring with laughter.

Emily withdrew early to seek repose, but her return to her native country and all the events and sufferings she had experienced since she had quitted it passed through her mind before she, at length, sank into sleep.

Lady Blanche was so much interested in Emily that she requested the Count would invite her to stay for some time at the château.

Emily, when she was recovered, wandered with her new friend over the grounds of the château. She perceived the towers of the convent that she wished to visit.

I AM BUT JUST RELEASED FROM A CONVENT. I NEVER FELT SO MUCH DEVOTION AS I DO HERE, WHERE I CAN WANDER FREELY.

When they returned to the château, Lady Blanche conducted Emily on a tour.

Emily was impressed by what she saw and she was interested in Dorothee, the housekeeper, who was very kind to her.

Emily had now been a week at the château. In one of the solitary hours, she unlocked a little box which contained some papers of her father and letters from Valancourt.

AH, MA'AMSELLE, YOU ARE SO YOUNG, SURELY YOU HAVE NOTHING SERIOUS TO GRIEVE YOU.

When Dorothee entered the room she hastily put up the papers.

NO, DOROTHEE; NOTHING OF ANY CONSEQUENCE.

HOLY MARY! WHAT IS IT I SEE? THAT *PICTURE!* IT IS MY BLESSED MISTRESS HERSELF!

IT IS BUT A MINIATURE I FOUND AMONGST MY FATHER'S PAPERS.

PLEASE TELL ME THE CAUSE OF YOUR GRIEF.

WELL, LADY, YOU SEEM MUCH INTERESTED. SO IF YOU PLEASE, I WILL COME BACK WHEN THE FAMILY ARE ALL IN BED.

In the evening the Count and his guests went to the woods to witness the festival of the peasants. Emily, lost in thought, strolled by herself and at length found herself near the avenue.

She had turned back when she heard steps approaching and distinguished the voice of Henri. Then an exclamation burst from the lips of his companion: it was Valancourt!

CAN IT BE? EMILY!

MY SUFFERINGS ARE ALL PASSED NOW!

Emily, with Valancourt, returned to the château where she presented him to the Count. The Count did not invite Valancourt to stay, so he retired to an inn for the night.

On the following day the Count joined Emily in one of her walks.

MAY I ASK HOW LONG YOU HAVE KNOWN MONSIEUR VALANCOURT?

"...I cannot but perceive that he admires you. But I feel obliged to inform you that the Chevalier's extravagance has brought him twice into prison in Paris whence he was extricated by a well-known Parisian Countess..."

...WITH WHOM HE CONTINUED TO RESIDE WHEN I LEFT PARIS!

The Count caught Emily as she fainted. When she revived she found herself supported, not by the Count, but by Valancourt.

O VALANCOURT! WE MUST PART, AND FOREVER! YOUR OWN CONDUCT HAS MADE THIS NECESSARY!

NO, EMILY! NO! YOU WOULD NOT SAY THIS IF YOU STILL LOVED ME!

PLEASE, DO NOT PROLONG THIS MOMENT BY A CONVERSATION. VALANCOURT, FAREWELL!

I WILL NOT DISTRESS YOU FURTHER. I AM GOING, EMILY – TO LEAVE YOU FOREVER!

It was long before Emily could sufficiently abstract her mind from Valancourt to listen to the story promised by Dorothee. It was after twelve when Dorothee's tap sounded at the door.

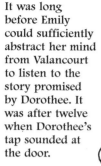

LET US SIT DOWN BY THIS WINDOW AND PRAY, DOROTHEE, AND IF IT IS NOT PAINFUL TO YOU, TELL ME SOMETHING ABOUT THE MARCHIONESS.

ALAS! WE ALL LOVED HER WELL. IT IS NOW MANY YEARS SINCE SHE DIED. POOR LADY! HOW GAY SHE WAS, WHEN SHE FIRST CAME TO THE CHÂTEAU!

AND WAS SHE NOT GAY AFTERWARDS?

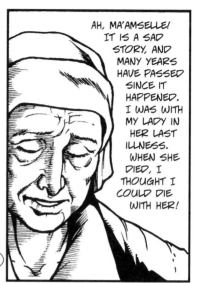

AH, MA'AMSELLE! IT IS A SAD STORY, AND MANY YEARS HAVE PASSED SINCE IT HAPPENED. I WAS WITH MY LADY IN HER LAST ILLNESS. WHEN SHE DIED, I THOUGHT I COULD DIE WITH HER!

"It is about twenty years since my lady the Marchioness came as a bride to the château. I well remember how she looked when she came into the great hall, and how happy my lord the Marquis seemed!"

"But my lady did not seem happy soon after the marriage. I found out that her father had commanded her to marry the Marquis for his money and there was another chevalier that she liked better."

"My lady always tried to conceal her tears from the Marquis, but my lord grew gloomy and very unkind to my lady."

"After matters had gone on thus for near a year, one night my lady was taken very ill. She desired I would call the Marquis, and tell him she had something particular to say to him."

"At last he came. My lady told him she felt herself to be dying. I left the room and I sent off a man for the doctor."

"When my lord came out of the bedroom, he went into his library and threw himself on the floor, and there he lay, and would hear no reason. I can hardly bear to think of it now!"

"She died in my arms, ma'amselle, and she went off as peacefully as child."

"When the doctor came he appeared greatly shocked to see her, for soon after her death a frightful blackness spread all over her face."

"He asked me several pointed questions and shook his head at my answers."

"Her apartments were sealed, and have never been opened since."

MY LORD THE MARQUIS DID NOT STAY LONG AT THE CHÂTEAU, BUT JOINED HIS REGIMENT. LATER WE HEARD THAT HE HAD DIED IN BATTLE.

THE DEATH OF THE MARCHIONESS APPEARS EXTRAORDINARY. BUT MAY WE NOW SEE HER APARTMENTS?

OH, *PLEASE* DON'T ASK ME THAT!

I AM TOLD THE COUNT INTENDS TO OPEN THAT WING IN THE NEXT WEEK.

THEN I SHOULD BE THE FIRST TO ENTER. IF YOU WILL MEET ME IN THE CORRIDOR OUTSIDE THE APARTMENTS AFTER THE DINNER IS CLEARED TONIGHT, I WILL OPEN THEM FOR YOU.

That afternoon saw the departure of Monsieur Du Pont. He bid an affectionate farewell to Emily and begged that she would allow him to visit her soon at La Vallée, a privilege she gladly consented.

Emily spent the remainder of the day in rising anticipation, and after the dinner hour she met Dorothee.

ALAS! THE LAST TIME I PASSED THOUGH THIS DOOR, I FOLLOWED MY POOR LADY'S CORPSE!

IT WAS IN *HERE* I SAT ON THAT TERRIBLE NIGHT, AND HELD MY LADY'S HAND – *HERE* SHE *DIED* IN MY ARMS!

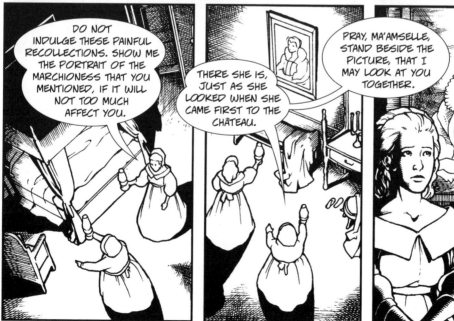

DO NOT INDULGE THESE PAINFUL RECOLLECTIONS. SHOW ME THE PORTRAIT OF THE MARCHIONESS THAT YOU MENTIONED, IF IT WILL NOT TOO MUCH AFFECT YOU.

THERE SHE IS, JUST AS SHE LOOKED WHEN SHE CAME FIRST TO THE CHÂTEAU.

PRAY, MA'AMSELLE, STAND BESIDE THE PICTURE, THAT I MAY LOOK AT YOU TOGETHER.

LET US GO, THE AIR OF THESE ROOMS IS UNWHOLESOME!

A LITTLE BEFORE MY LADY'S DEATH, I SAT DOWN JUST THERE, HOW WELL I REMEMBER HER LOOK AT THE TIME— *DEATH* WAS IN IT!

IT IS ONLY THE *WIND* THAT WAVES IT. WE HAVE LEFT ALL THE DOORS OPEN— IT IS ONLY THE *WIND*!

EEEEEEEEEEEEEEHHHHHHH!

AAAAAAAAAHHHHHHHHHHH!!!

The women fled as fast as their trembling limbs would bear them. When they reached the staircase, Dorothee opened a chamber door, where some of the servants slept.

When she could finally speak, she affected to laugh at her own fright, and was joined by Emily.

Dorothee recollected that she had left the doors of the rooms open, and not having courage to return alone, Emily accompanied her.

They were joined by Annette, who was so terrified by the reports of the servants that Emily consented that she should stay in her room for the night.

Emily's injunctions to Annette to be silent on the subject of her terror were ineffectual, and the occurrence of the preceding night quickly spread among the staff. A report soon reached the Count of the north side of the castle being haunted. He forbade any person to repeat it.

The arrival of a party of the Count's friends soon withdrew his thoughts from this subject.

Among the visitors was the Baron de Saint Foix and his son the Chevalier St. Foix, who, having met the Lady Blanche the preceding year, had become her admirer.

While these visitors were at the château their joy was only dampened by a growing alarm among the servants.

Several of them determined to leave the château, and requested their discharge of the Count.

It was now that Ludovico proved his gratitude for the kindness he had received from the Count, by offering to watch, during the night, in the suite reputed to be haunted.

Annette employed tears and entreaties to dissuade him from his purpose.

YOUR INTREPIDITY SHALL NOT GO UNREWARDED. YOU SHALL HAVE A SWORD, AND YOUR **BRAVE** COMRADES MAY FIND COURAGE ENOUGH FROM YOUR EXAMPLE TO REMAIN ANOTHER NIGHT IN THE CHÂTEAU!

Curiosity now struggled with fear in the minds of his fellow servants and they resolved to await the results of Ludovico's rashness.

That evening the Count led the way to the door of the north apartments, followed by most of the inhabitants of the château.

As the door was opened, Dorothee uttered a sudden shriek and retreated, as did the other servants.

EEEEK!

The Count, Henri and Ludovico proceeded through the salon and into the bedroom.

IF YOU DOUBT OF THIS, LUDOVICO, DO NOT BE ASHAMED TO OWN IT, AND I WILL RELEASE YOU FROM YOUR ENGAGEMENT.

NO, MY LORD, I WILL GO THROUGH WITH WHAT I HAVE BEGUN. WITH A FIRE, THE GOOD CHEER IN THIS BASKET AND A BOOK TO ENTERTAIN ME, I DOUBT NOT THAT I SHALL DO WELL.

WELL, I HOPE NOTHING WILL DISTURB YOU. TOMORROW, I SHALL HAVE TO THANK YOU FOR AN IMPORTANT SERVICE.

Ludovico bid them goodnight and fastened the door to the apartments. Then he returned to the bedroom.

When he had finished his repast, he began to read, and his attention was soon wholly occupied by the scenes which the pages disclosed. Thus he passed the long hours.

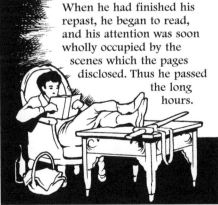

In the morning the Count rose early and, anxious to speak with Ludovico, went to the north apartments. Neither the knocking at the locked door nor his voice were heard.

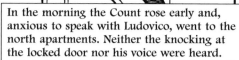

KNOCK... KNOCK... KNOCK...

LUDOVICO! LUDOVICO! HE SLEEPS SOUNDLY! TO GAIN ADMITTANCE IT WILL BE NECESSARY TO FORCE THE LOCK.

LUDOVICO! LUDOVICO!

A servant forced the door and the Count and Henri entered, while the others awaited the results of the enquiry on the landing.

Everything remained as on the preceding night. But Ludovico was nowhere to be found.

The most strenuous search after Ludovico proved unsuccessful.

LUDOVICO!

Poor Annette gave herself up to despair. Many of the servants quit the mansion immediately, and the rest remained only until replacements could be procured.

Emily, desirous of the quiet of the convent of St. Claire, determined that day to make her much-delayed visit. At the convent she was welcomed by the Abbess, and she once more wept over her father's grave.

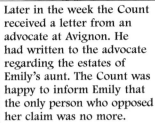

Later in the week the Count received a letter from an advocate at Avignon. He had written to the advocate regarding the estates of Emily's aunt. The Count was happy to inform Emily that the only person who opposed her claim was no more.

Montoni's depredations had reached an extent which the senate of Venice would not permit to continue. A corps of considerable strength had been sent to Udolpho.

Montoni and his colleagues were captured and returned to prison in Venice. There, it was said, he had died in a mysterious manner.

The Count called on Emily at the convent, to inform her it was now necessary for her to lay claim to the estates of her late aunt. Emily assured the Count of the pleasure with which she should have him as her guest at La Vallée.

The Count took his leave, and Emily joined a group of nuns in conversation. She was surprised to find them acquainted with events in the château, and with the count's efforts to find the missing Ludovico.

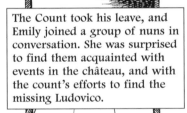

THE **GUILTY** CANNOT CLAIM HIS PROTECTION! YOU ARE YET INNOCENT OF ANY CRIME! BUT YOU HAVE **SCORPIONS** IN YOUR HEART—THEY SLEEP NOW— **BEWARE** YOU AWAKEN THEM!

MY HEAD **BURNS!** I BELIEVE I AM NOT WELL! O, COULD I STRIKE FROM MY MEMORY **ALL** FORMER SCENES! I SEE THEM NOW—**NOW!**

DO NOT BE ALARMED, OUR SISTER OFTEN IS THUS DERANGED. THIS FIT HAS BEEN COMING ON FOR SEVERAL DAYS.

DO YOU KNOW WHAT CIRCUMSTANCE REDUCED HER TO THIS DEPLORABLE CONDITION?

I CANNOT TELL YOU NOW, BUT COME TO MY CELL TONIGHT WHEN OUR SISTERHOOD ARE AT REST AND YOU SHALL HEAR MORE.

When the nuns had retired to rest, Emily stole to her appointment with Sister Frances.

I SHALL CONSIDER YOUR CONFIDENCE IN ME A FAVOR AND WILL NOT MISUSE IT.

"Sister Agnes is of a noble family. Love was the occasion of her crime, and of her madness. Her father secreted her in this convent, where she took vows before the Archbishop. A report was circulated in the world that she was dead."

BY WHAT MEANS DID HE THIS?

I NEVER COULD LEARN: THIS CONVENT HAS BEEN HER PLACE OF REFUGE FOR AS MANY YEARS AS MAKE YOUR AGE!

IT WAS ABOUT THAT SAME PERIOD THAT THE MARCHIONESS DE VILLEROI EXPIRED!

HOW STRANGE THAT YOU SHOULD REMARK THAT...

Several days followed during which Emily saw neither the Count nor any of his family. When he next appeared his air was unusually disturbed.

I AM VERY ANXIOUS ABOUT LUDOVICO. EVERY PART OF THE CHÂTEAU HAS BEEN SEARCHED, AND I KNOW NOT WHAT FURTHER CAN BE DONE.

I MEAN TO CHANGE MY RESIDENCE FOR A LITTLE WHILE. MY DAUGHTER AND I WILL ACCOMPANY THE BARON ST. FOIX TO HIS CHÂTEAU, AFTER WHICH I HOPE, EMILY, THAT WE MAY VISIT YOU IN YOUR HOME...

IT IS UNNECESSARY TO SAY WITH WHAT PLEASURE I SHOULD RECEIVE YOU AND THE LADY BLANCHE AT LA VALLÉE.

Early the next day Emily set out for Toulouse, attended by the unhappy Annette. She had spent a week arranging her late aunt's affairs, when Annette brought news.

LAST NIGHT, MA'AMSELLE, THERE WAS A *ROBBER* IN THE GARDEN!

THE GARDENER *FIRED* AT HIM, BUT WHEN HE WENT IN THE MORNING TO LOOK FOR THE BODY, IT WAS *GONE!*

Annette was interrupted: for as Emily envisioned the possibility of the man being Valancourt, her spirit died away and she would have fallen to the ground if the girl had not caught her.

Emily was reluctant to leave Toulouse without learning the identity of the intruder in the garden.

But a letter from Lady Blanche informed her that she and the Count intended to visit La Vallée on their way home.

On the following morning Emily left Toulouse and reached La Vallée about sunset.

One of her earliest inquires was concerning Theresa, her father's old servant. She now lived in a cottage near La Vallée.

MY DEAR YOUNG LADY, I THOUGHT I SHOULD NEVER SEE YOU AGAIN! AND HOW DOES MONSIEUR VALANCOURT? DID YOU KNOW HE GAVE ME THIS COTTAGE?

VALANCOURT! H-HOW LONG IS IT SINCE YOU HAVE SEEN HIM?

NOT THIS MANY A DAY... WHY, YOU ARE *TREMBLING!* IT *IS* A COLD EVENING. DO TAKE THIS CHAIR BY THE HEARTH...

Emily burst into tears at the thought of the man shot in the garden.

At the same time, at the Château de St. Foix, the Count De Villefort and Lady Blanche bade adieu to the Baron and Baroness, with the hope of seeing them soon.

For it was settled that Monsieur St. Foix should receive the hand of the Lady Blanche upon their return to Château-le-Blanc.

As the road from the Baron's residence to La Vallée was over some of the wildest tract of the Pyrenees, the Count hired mules for himself and his family. After a day's journey, the travelers found themselves in a woody valley. Blanche viewed the scenery in silence and a growing apprehension.

The shadow of evening soon shifted to the gloom of night, and the guides reluctantly confessed that they had lost their way. Finally, they were cheered by the bark of a dog. A light was seen to glimmer at a distance and voices were heard.

NUMEROUS FORTS AND WATCHTOWERS HAVE BEEN ERECTED AMONG THE PYRENEES. NOW THEY ARE CONVERTED INTO THE MORE PEACEFUL HABITATIONS OF HUNTERS AND SHEPHERDS, THOUGH SOMETIMES THEY ARE THE ASYLUM OF FRENCH AND SPANISH SMUGGLERS...

BANG! BANG!

WE ARE *FRIENDS*, WHO ASK SHELTER FOR THE NIGHT!

In a few moments, the gate slowly opened, and several men appeared and told him he was welcome.

WE ARE TRAVELERS, BUT IF YOU WILL ADMIT US TO YOUR HUNTER'S FARE, WE SHALL BE WELL CONTENTED, AND WILL REPAY YOUR KINDNESS.

SIT DOWN THEN, BROTHER. THE FOOD WILL SOON BE READY. JACQUES, LAY MORE FUEL ON THE FIRE! AND BRING A SEAT FOR THE LADY, TOO!

The Count was asking of their success at hunting when a horn sounded at the gate.

THE LIFE OF A HUNTER IS A PLEASANT AND HEALTHY ONE, AND THE REPOSE IS SWEET WHICH SUCCEEDS TO YOUR LABOR.

YES, OUR LIFE IS PLEASANT ENOUGH. WE LIVE HERE ONLY DURING THE SUMMER AND AUTUMNAL MONTHS.

THESE ARE SOME OF OUR COMPANIONS, RETURNED FROM THE HUNT.

WHAT *CHEER*, MY LADS? WHO THE DEVIL HAVE *YOU* BROUGHT HOME?

THIS CHEVALIER AND HIS PARTY HAVE LOST THEIR WAY, AND ASK A NIGHT'S LODGING IN THE FORT.

The Count noticed a suspicious glitter in the hunter's heavy sack.

THERE IS DANGER HERE! PASS THE WORD TO THE MEN TO KEEP THEIR ARMS READY!

A figure crept from the shadows…

DO NOT DRINK THE WINE! IT IS *POISONED!*

With a start, the Count recognized the voice of Ludovico! One of the men noticed the exchange and drew his knife menacingly.

TREACHERY! DEFEND YOURSELVES!

A violent struggle ensued, but at last the Count's men prevailed, and the surviving attackers were locked in the fort's dungeon.

THE BANDITTI THAT ARE STILL OUT, MY LORD, WERE EXPECTED HOME A HOUR AGO, AND THEY WILL CERTAINLY OUTNUMBER US!

The Count decided it was best to leave at once, despite St. Foix's severe wounds. He was carefully placed on a stretcher made of bear's skin and carried by the guides.

As they passed along the hall, a loud tumult was heard and Blanche was terrified.

IT IS ONLY THOSE VILLAINS IN THE DUNGEON, MY LADY. WE HAVE NOTHING TO FEAR FROM THEM, BUT WE MUST BEWARE THEIR COMPANIONS!

Ludovico led the way, and the party soon found themselves in a narrow valley. They pressed on and finally the exhausted travelers arrived at the inn where they had designed to pass the preceding night.

I HAVE SEEN HIS *GHOST*, MA'AMSELLE!

WHO DO YOU MEAN?

LUDOVICO! IT IS LUDOVICO!

In a few minutes Ludovico appeared, to the delight of both Emily and Annette.

He delivered letters from the Count de Villefort and Lady Blanche informing her of their intent to visit on the next day.

Emily asked Ludovico to explain his disappearance from Château-le-Blanc.

THAT NIGHT, SIGNORA, AFTER THE COUNT AND MONSIEUR HENRI LEFT ME IN THE NORTH CHAMBER, I HAD SAT READING FOR SOME HOURS WHEN I FELT DROWSY...

"I was awakened by a noise, and when I looked up, I saw the arras near the bed slowly lifted. A man appeared, then I saw the face of another man behind him!"

"Though my sword was upon the table before me, I had not the power to seize it. I sat quite still watching them, with my eyes half-shut as if I was asleep."

"They all rushed into the room and surrounded me."

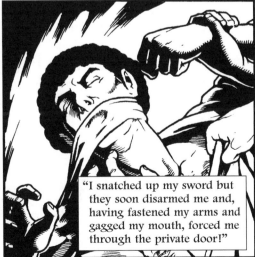

"I snatched up my sword but they soon disarmed me and, having fastened my arms and gagged my mouth, forced me through the private door!"

"They led me through many narrow passages and down steps 'til we came into a cave. We walked through to the mouth of it, and I found myself on the beach at the foot of the cliff, with the château above."

"The ruffians forced me into a boat and we soon reached a small sailing vessel."

"We landed at Rousillon, and they carried me with them to the fort in the mountains."

"I soon found out that they were pirates…"

"They had during many years secreted their spoil in the vault of the castle, which, being so near the sea, suited their purpose well."

"The cave was open to anybody and their treasures would not long have remained undiscovered there."

"To prevent detection they had tried to have it believed that the château was haunted, and having discovered the private way to the north apartment they easily succeeded. A report soon went abroad that it was haunted."

THIS IS AN EXTRAORDINARY ADVENTURE, LUDOVICO. DID YOU EVER HEAR THE BANDITTI RELATE ANYTHING UNUSUAL OF THE NORTH ROOMS?

NO SIGNORA, EXCEPT ONE OF THE PIRATES MENTIONED THE CREDULITY OF THE COUNT'S MAIDS. ONE NIGHT IN THE BEDROOM, HE HEARD SOMEBODY APPROACHING…

NOT HAVING TIME TO ESCAPE THROUGH THE DOOR, HE HID HIMSELF IN THE BED…

"…and, thinking that his only chance of escaping was by terrifying them, lifted up the counterpane. They both set off as if they had seen the devil!"

Emily could not forbear smiling in embarrassment at this explanation.

On the following morning, the arrival of her friend revived Emily's spirits. The unfortunate adventure in the Pyrenees had made the Count very anxious to return home, so Emily prepared to set out with her friends for Languedoc.

There she would attend the wedding of the Lady Blanche and Monsieur St. Foix.

On the third evening of her arrival at the Château-le-Blanc, Emily decided to visit the Abbess and her friends among the nuns.

Accompanied by Blanche, she walked to the monastery.

In the great hall an unusual silence seemed to reign. The Abbess entered the hall, her manner unusually solemn.

OUR DAUGHTER AGNES IS DYING. I LEFT HER WITH HER CONFESSOR AND A GENTLEMAN.

DURING HER ILLNESS SHE HAS SOMETIMES NAMED YOU, AND PERHAPS IT WOULD COMFORT HER TO SEE YOU.

The Abbess conducted her to an apartment. There was laid sister Agnes.

AH! IT IS HER VERY *SELF!* WHAT *IS* IT YOU COME TO DEMAND? *RETRIBUTION?* WHAT ARE YEARS OF PRAYERS AND REPENTANCE?

TELL ME, ARE YOU THE *DAUGHTER* OF THE MARCHIONESS DE VILLEROI? BRING ME THAT CASKET, SISTER, I WILL *PROVE* IT TO YOU!

Emily perceived the exact resemblance of the picture she had found among her father's papers.

THERE IS *ANOTHER* PICTURE I WOULD SHOW TO YOU.

LOOK WELL AT THIS PICTURE AND SEE IF YOU CAN DISCOVER ANY RESEMBLANCE BETWEEN WHAT I WAS AND WHAT I AM! YES — *I AM SIGNORA LAURENTINI!*

Emily received the miniature in her trembling hands.

85

YOU DISAPPEARED... AT *UDOLPHO*.

YOU HAVE *BEEN* AT UDOLPHO THEN! THAT WHICH WAS ONCE *MINE!*

WHAT SCENES DOES THE MENTION OF IT REVIVE IN MY FANCY; SCENES OF *HAPPINESS* — OF *SUFFERING* — AND OF *HORROR!*

THE WEST CHAMBER — THE MOURNFUL *VEIL* — THE OBJECT IT *CONCEALS*...

YOU COME FROM THE GRAVE!

Sister Agnes fell into convulsions and Emily hurried from the room in horror. In the dying nun she had discovered Signora Laurentini, who was herself guilty of a dreadful crime.

As the ladies returned to the château, Blanche pointed out two persons advancing on the dusky path. Emily distinguished the voice of Henri, and his companion was the gentleman whom she had seen at the monastery: Monsieur Bonnac, a distant relative of Signora Laurentini, who had been called on to execute her will.

The Count, when he heard of the presence of Monsieur Bonnac, claimed him for an acquaintance and invited him to stay.

Monsieur Bonnac had recently been confined for several months in one of the prisons of Paris, due to the pecuniary extravagance of his son.

ONE GENEROUS FRIEND, WHO WAS IN CONFINEMENT AT THE SAME TIME, EMPLOYED THE FIRST MOMENTS OF HIS LIBERTY IN EFFORTS TO OBTAIN MINE. AH! AMIABLE AND UNFORTUNATE VALANCOURT!

M. Bonnac revealed that Valancourt had been drawn into vice by his fellow officers. He had lost large sums, to which the Count de Villefort had been witness.

In consequence of accumulated debts, Valancourt was thrown into confinement.

After his release by his brother from the prison, Valancourt realized that he had thrown away the fortune without which he could never hope to marry Emily.

He made a solemn vow never again to yield to the destructive vice of gaming.

When the Count was informed of the error he had committed regarding Valancourt's character he immediately wrote to invite him to Château-le-Blanc.

A few days following that on which Signora Laurentini died, her will was opened. It was found that one third of her personal property was bequeathed to the nearest surviving relative of the late Marchioness de Villeroi…

…and that Emily was that person!

The Abbess, due to the extraordinary confession of Signora Laurentini in her dying hours, felt it necessary to reveal the truth to her young friend.

Emily learned that the Marchioness de Villeroi had been the sister of M. St Aubert.

And then the Abbess told her the story of Sister Agnes, who was known to the world as Signora Laurentini.

She was the heiress of the ancient house of Udolpho, and mistress of all the arts of fascination. Among her admirers was the late Marquis de Villeroi.

Having passed some weeks at Udolpho, he was called abruptly to France.

Several months passed. At length, a report reached her that the Marquis had married in France. She formed the desperate resolution of going secretly to that country.

One night, with only one servant, she left Udolpho for France.

Once she was with him, the Marquis was not proof against her beauty. The artful Italian had regained such influence over the Marquis that finally he consented to destroy his wife.

A slow poison was administered, and the Marchioness fell victim to the jealousy of Laurentini and to the weakness of her husband.

THE PASSION OF REVENGE SOON DIED AND LEFT SIGNORA LAURENTINI TO THE HORRORS OF REMORSE: SHE RENOUNCED THE WORLD. THE MARQUIS, BURDENED WITH HIS GUILT, QUITTED CHÂTEAU-LE-BLANC, TO WHICH HE NEVER RETURNED.

I BELIEVED THAT I SAW THE **MURDERED BODY** OF THE LADY LAURENTINI BEHIND THE **BLACK VEIL** AT UDOLPHO!

"I have heard something of this. A penance was designed by the Church to reprove the pride of the Marquis of Udolpho."

"A waxen image was stationed in a wall, and the Marquis was condemned to contemplate it daily, as a pardon for his sins."

The mysteries of Udolpho were solved!

Emily remained some weeks at the Château-le-Blanc, awaiting the nuptials of the Lady Blanche. One evening, having wandered with her lute to her favorite spot near the shore, she entered a room in the ruined tower.

AH, EMILY! HAVE I NO *HOPE?*

WHEN YOU CEASED TO *ESTEEM* ME, DID YOU ALSO CEASE TO *LOVE* ME?

MY *DEAR* VALANCOURT...!

I WAS IGNORANT OF ALL THE CIRCUMSTANCES OF YOUR CONDUCT, BUT THOUGH I CEASED TO ESTEEM, I HAD *NEVER* FORGOTTEN YOU!

I *AM DEAR* TO YOU THEN—*STILL* DEAR TO YOU, MY EMILY!

Valancourt described his recovery from the wound he had received in the gardens at Toulouse. Since then, he had worked to clear his debts and restore his damaged reputation.

The Count greeted Valancourt cordially, and granted him his blessing for the future happiness of Emily.

The marriages of the Lady Blanche and Emily St. Aubert were celebrated on the same day at Château-le-Blanc.

Oh, useful may it be to have shown, that though the vicious can pour affliction upon the good, their power is transient and their punishment certain; and that innocence, though oppressed by injustice, shall finally triumph over misfortune! And, if the weak hand that has recorded this tale has beguiled the mourner of one hour of sorrow, or taught him to sustain it — the effort, however humble, has not been vain, nor is the writer unrewarded.

Ann Radcliffe, 1794

EDGAR ALLAN POE'S

THE OVAL PORTRAIT

adapted by
TOM POMPLUN

illustrated by
LEONG WAN KOK

THE CHATEAU INTO WHICH MY VALET HAD VENTURED TO MAKE FORCIBLE ENTRANCE, RATHER THAN PERMIT ME, IN MY WEAKENED CONDITION, TO PASS A NIGHT IN THE OPEN AIR, WAS ONE OF THOSE PILES OF COMMINGLED GLOOM AND GRANDEUR WHICH HAVE SO LONG FROWNED AMONG THE APENNINES....

...NOT LESS IN FACT THAN IN THE FANCY OF MRS. RADCLIFFE. TO ALL APPEARANCE THE PLACE HAD BEEN TEMPORARILY AND VERY LATELY ABANDONED. WE ESTABLISHED OURSELVES IN ONE OF THE SMALLEST AND LEAST SUMPTUOUSLY FURNISHED APARTMENTS. IT LAY IN A REMOTE TURRET OF THE BUILDING.

THE ROOM'S DECORATIONS WERE RICH, YET TATTERED AND ANTIQUE, AND INCLUDED AN UNUSUALLY GREAT NUMBER OF MODERN PAINTINGS, FRAMED IN RICH GOLDEN ARABESQUE.

IT WAS, PERHAPS, MY INCIPIENT DELIRIUM WHICH CAUSED ME TO TAKE SUCH A DEEP INTEREST IN THE PAINTINGS.

I BADE PEDRO TO LIGHT A CANDELABRA AND PLACE IT BY THE HEAD OF MY BED BEFORE HE RETIRED. I WISHED TO RESIGN MYSELF, IF NOT TO SLEEP, AT LEAST ALTERNATELY TO THE CONTEMPLATION OF THE PICTURES....

...AND THE PERUSAL OF A SMALL VOLUME WHICH DESCRIBED THEM, AND WHICH I HAD FOUND NEXT TO THE BED.

LONG — LONG I READ — AND DEVOUTLY, DEVOTEDLY I GAZED, AS THE DEEP MIDNIGHT CAME AND MY VALET SLUMBERED IN PEACE.

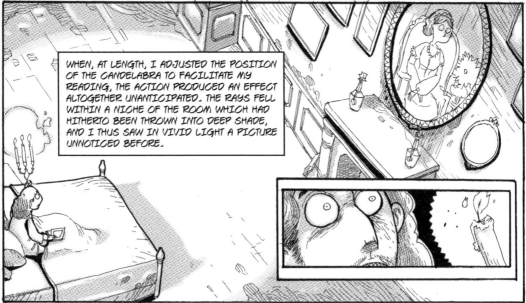

WHEN, AT LENGTH, I ADJUSTED THE POSITION OF THE CANDELABRA TO FACILITATE MY READING, THE ACTION PRODUCED AN EFFECT ALTOGETHER UNANTICIPATED. THE RAYS FELL WITHIN A NICHE OF THE ROOM WHICH HAD HITHERTO BEEN THROWN INTO DEEP SHADE, AND I THUS SAW IN VIVID LIGHT A PICTURE UNNOTICED BEFORE.

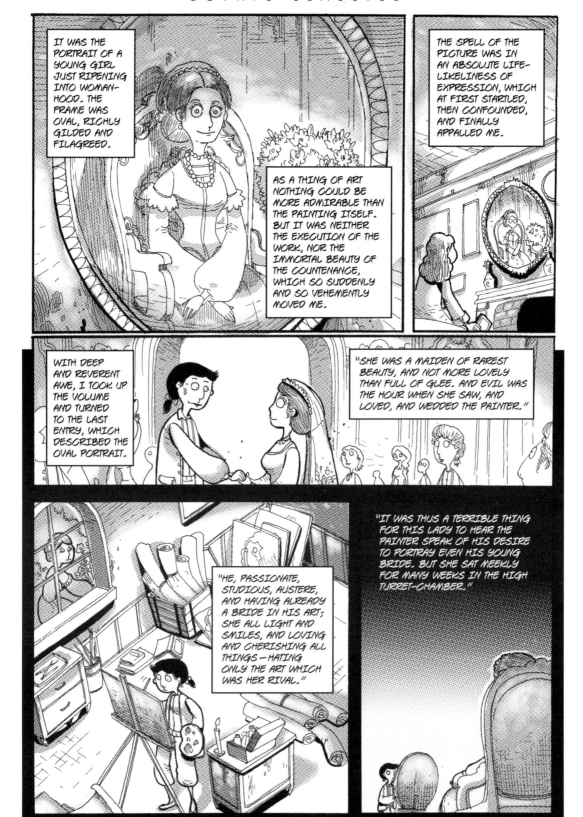

IT WAS THE PORTRAIT OF A YOUNG GIRL JUST RIPENING INTO WOMAN-HOOD. THE FRAME WAS OVAL, RICHLY GILDED AND FILAGREED.

AS A THING OF ART NOTHING COULD BE MORE ADMIRABLE THAN THE PAINTING ITSELF. BUT IT WAS NEITHER THE EXECUTION OF THE WORK, NOR THE IMMORTAL BEAUTY OF THE COUNTENANCE, WHICH SO SUDDENLY AND SO VEHEMENTLY MOVED ME.

THE SPELL OF THE PICTURE WAS IN AN ABSOLUTE LIFE-LIKELINESS OF EXPRESSION, WHICH AT FIRST STARTLED, THEN CONFOUNDED, AND FINALLY APPALLED ME.

WITH DEEP AND REVERENT AWE, I TOOK UP THE VOLUME AND TURNED TO THE LAST ENTRY, WHICH DESCRIBED THE OVAL PORTRAIT.

"SHE WAS A MAIDEN OF RAREST BEAUTY, AND NOT MORE LOVELY THAN FULL OF GLEE. AND EVIL WAS THE HOUR WHEN SHE SAW, AND LOVED, AND WEDDED THE PAINTER."

"HE, PASSIONATE, STUDIOUS, AUSTERE, AND HAVING ALREADY A BRIDE IN HIS ART; SHE ALL LIGHT AND SMILES, AND LOVING AND CHERISHING ALL THINGS — HATING ONLY THE ART WHICH WAS HER RIVAL."

"IT WAS THUS A TERRIBLE THING FOR THIS LADY TO HEAR THE PAINTER SPEAK OF HIS DESIRE TO PORTRAY EVEN HIS YOUNG BRIDE. BUT SHE SAT MEEKLY FOR MANY WEEKS IN THE HIGH TURRET-CHAMBER."

"THE PAINTER TOOK GLORY IN HIS WORK, WHICH WENT ON FROM HOUR TO HOUR AND FROM DAY TO DAY. HE COULD NOT SEE THAT THE LIGHT WHICH FELL SO GHASTLILY IN THAT LONE TURRET WITHERED THE HEALTH AND THE SPIRITS OF HIS BRIDE."

"YET, SHE SMILED ON, AND GREW DAILY MORE DISPIRITED AND WEAK."

"AS THE LABOR DREW NEARER TO ITS CONCLUSION, THE PAINTER GREW WILD WITH THE ARDOR OF HIS WORK, AND TURNED HIS EYES FROM THE CANVAS RARELY, EVEN TO REGARD THE COUNTENANCE OF HIS WIFE."

"AND WHEN MANY WEEKS HAD PASSED, THE FINAL STROKE AT LAST WAS PLACED."

"THE PAINTER STOOD ENTRANCED BEFORE THE WORK WHICH HE HAD WROUGHT."

THIS IS INDEED LIFE ITSELF!

"BUT WHILE HE YET GAZED HE GREW AGHAST. HE TURNED SUDDENLY TO REGARD HIS BELOVED —"

"SHE WAS DEAD!"

93

JANE AUSTEN's Northanger Abbey

adapted by *TRINA ROBBINS*   illustrated by *ANNE TIMMONS*

NO ONE WHO HAD EVER SEEN CATHERINE MORLAND AT TEN WOULD HAVE SUPPOSED HER BORN TO BE A **HEROINE**. HER FATHER WAS A VERY RESPECTABLE CLERGYMAN WHO WAS NOT IN THE **LEAST** ADDICTED TO LOCKING UP HIS DAUGHTERS.

HER MOTHER HAD THREE SONS BEFORE CATHERINE WAS BORN, AND INSTEAD OF DYING WHEN THE LATTER WAS BORN, LIVED ON TO HAVE SIX MORE, TO SEE THEM GROWING UP, AND TO ENJOY EXCELLENT HEALTH.

CATHERINE HAD REACHED THE AGE OF SEVENTEEN WITHOUT HAVING INSPIRED ONE REAL PASSION.

SIGH...

THERE WAS NOT *ONE* LORD IN THE NEIGHBORHOOD OF FULLERTON; NO — NOT EVEN A BARONET. THERE WAS NOT *ONE* FAMILY AMONG THEIR ACQUAINTANCE WHO HAD REARED A BOY ACCIDENTALLY FOUND AT THEIR DOOR.

BUT WHEN A YOUNG LADY IS TO BE A HEROINE, SOMETHING *MUST* AND *WILL* HAPPEN TO THROW A HERO IN HER WAY.

MR. ALLEN, WHO OWNED THE CHIEF OF THE PROPERTY IN FULLERTON, WHERE CATHERINE'S FAMILY LIVED, WAS ORDERED TO THE HOT SPRINGS OF BATH FOR THE BENEFIT OF A GOUTY DISPOSITION.

...SO PERHAPS YOU WOULD LIKE TO COME WITH US, MY DEAR, TO VISIT THE CELEBRATED RESORT CITY.

OH, MRS. ALLEN, I SHOULD *LOVE* TO!

CATHERINE'S JOURNEY TO BATH WAS PERFORMED WITH UNEVENTFUL SAFETY. NEITHER ROBBERS NOR TEMPEST BEFRIENDED THEM, NOR ONE LUCKY OVERTURN TO INTRODUCE THEM TO THE HERO, AND SOON THEY WERE SETTLED IN COMFORTABLE LODGINGS.

AT THE BATHS, THE UPPER ROOM WAS CROWDED AND THE TWO LADIES SQUEEZED IN AS WELL AS THEY COULD. MR. ALLEN REPAIRED DIRECTLY TO THE CARD ROOM AND LEFT THEM TO ENJOY THE MOB BY THEMSELVES.

I *WISH* YOU COULD DANCE, MY DEAR.

SIGH...

I *WISH* YOU COULD GET A PARTNER.

BY UNWEARIED DILIGENCE THEY GAINED THE TOP OF THE ROOM WHERE CATHERINE BEGAN, FOR THE FIRST TIME, TO FEEL HERSELF AT A BALL.

SHE LONGED TO DANCE, BUT SHE HAD NOT AN ACQUAINTANCE IN THE ROOM.

WHEN THE DANCE WAS OVER, THEY WERE JOINED BY MR. ALLEN.

WELL, MISS MORLAND, I HOPE YOU HAVE HAD AN AGREEABLE BALL.

VERY AGREEABLE, INDEED.

I SAY...

THERE'S A DEUCED PRETTY GIRL.

!

THE NEXT DAY, FORTUNE WAS MORE FAVORABLE TO OUR HEROINE — THE MASTER OF CEREMONIES INTRODUCED HER TO A YOUNG MAN AS A DANCING PARTNER.

CATHERINE WAS PLEASED TO FIND HE WAS A CLERGYMAN, OF A VERY RESPECTABLE FAMILY IN GLOUCESTERSHIRE.

DO COME ALONG, DEAR.

WHEN THE ASSEMBLY CLOSED, THEY PARTED, ON THE LADY'S SIDE AT LEAST, WITH A STRONG INCLINATION FOR CONTINUING THE ACQUAINTANCE.

SIGH...

WHETHER SHE DREAMED OF HIM THAT NIGHT CANNOT BE ASCERTAINED; BUT SHE KNEW IT MUST BE VERY IMPROPER THAT A YOUNG LADY SHOULD DREAM OF A GENTLEMAN BEFORE THE GENTLEMAN IS FIRST KNOWN TO HAVE DREAMT OF HER.

WITH MORE THAN USUAL EAGERNESS DID CATHERINE HASTEN TO THE PUMP ROOM THE NEXT DAY, BUT MR. TILNEY DID NOT APPEAR.

WHAT A **DELIGHTFUL** PLACE BATH IS...

...AND HOW **PLEASANT** IT WOULD BE IF WE HAD ANY ACQUAINTANCE HERE.

SIGH...

HARDLY HAD THEY BEEN SEATED TEN MINUTES BEFORE A LADY ADDRESSED MRS. ALLEN.

I THINK, MADAM, I **CANNOT** BE MISTAKEN; IT IS A LONG TIME SINCE I HAD THE PLEASURE OF SEEING YOU, BUT IS NOT YOUR NAME **ALLEN**?

MRS. ALLEN RECOGNIZED A FORMER SCHOOLMATE, WHOM SHE HAD LAST SEEN MANY YEARS AGO. MRS. THORPE WAS A WIDOW, AND NOT A VERY RICH ONE. SHE, HOWEVER, HAD ONE GREAT ADVANTAGE OVER MRS. ALLEN, WHEN SHE EXPIATED ON THE TALENTS OF HER SON, AND THE BEAUTY OF HER DAUGHTER.

HERE COMES MY DEAR ISABELLA!

MISS THORPE WAS INTRODUCED; AND MISS MORLAND WAS INTRODUCED LIKEWISE.

HOW **EXCESSIVELY** LIKE HER BROTHER MISS MORLAND IS!

THE **VERY PICTURE** OF HIM INDEED! I SHOULD HAVE KNOWN HER **ANYWHERE** FOR HIS SISTER!

CATHERINE REMEMBERED THAT HER OLDEST BROTHER HAD LATELY FORMED AN INTIMACY WITH A YOUNG MAN NAMED THORPE, AND HAD SPENT CHRISTMAS VACATION WITH HIS FAMILY, NEAR LONDON.

WE SHALL BE **GREAT** FRIENDS!

WELL, I...

TELL ME, WHAT **DO** YOU THINK OF THE NEW MUSLINS FROM PARIS?

I HAD SOME SPRIGGED COTTON MADE UP INTO THE MOST **CUNNING** DRESS.

YOU **MUST** SEE IT!

CATHERINE FELT GRATEFUL FOR THE CHANCE THAT HAD PROCURED HER SUCH A FRIEND AS MISS THORPE, BUT SHE DID NOT FORGET TO LOOK FOR MR. TILNEY.

...AND I THOUGHT THE LACE ON HER PELISSE WAS NOT *HALF* SO HANDSOME AS THAT ON MY *OWN*.

BUT SHE LOOKED IN VAIN. HE WAS NOWHERE TO BE MET WITH, AND HE MUST BE GONE FROM BATH.

CATHERINE AND ISABELLA WERE ALWAYS ARM IN ARM WHEN THEY WALKED, AND IF A RAINY MORNING DEPRIVED THEM OF OTHER ENJOYMENTS, THEY SHUT THEMSELVES UP TO READ NOVELS TOGETHER.

OH! I FEAR I SHALL NOT SLEEP TONIGHT! THIS BOOK, *UDOLPHO*, IS SIMPLY *HORRID*!

IS IT NOT? *SIMPLY, DELICIOUSLY* HORRID!

MY DEAREST CATHERINE, WHAT **HAVE** YOU BEEN DOING WITH YOURSELF ALL MORNING?

ONE MORNING CATHERINE KEPT A RENDEZVOUS WITH ISABELLA IN THE PUMP ROOM.

OH! I WOULD NOT TELL YOU WHAT IS BEHIND THE BLACK VEIL FOR THE **WORLD!** ARE YOU NOT **WILD** TO KNOW?

HAVE YOU BEEN READING **UDOLPHO?**

YES, I HAVE BEEN READING IT EVER SINCE I WOKE, AND HAVE GOTTEN TO THE BLACK VEIL.

WHEN YOU HAVE FINISHED **UDOLPHO,** I HAVE MADE OUT A LIST OF TEN OR TWELVE **MORE** FOR YOU.

YES, BUT WHAT CAN IT BE? I AM **SURE** IT IS LAURENTINA'S **SKELETON!**

HAVE YOU, INDEED! AND ARE YOU SURE THEY ARE ALL **HORRID?**

YES, QUITE SURE, **DELICIOUSLY HORRID!**

OH! LET US MOVE AWAY FROM THIS END OF THE ROOM...

...THERE ARE TWO **ODIOUS** YOUNG MEN WHO HAVE BEEN **STARING** AT ME THIS HALF HOUR.

MY DEAR ISABELLA, YOU NEED NO LONGER BE UNEASY, AS THE GENTLEMEN HAVE **LEFT** THE PUMP ROOM.

AND WHICH **WAY** ARE THEY **GONE?**

THEY WENT TOWARDS THE CHURCHYARD.

WELL, I AM **GLAD** TO HAVE GOTTEN RID OF THEM. NOW, WHAT SAY YOU TO GOING TO LOOK AT MY NEW HAT?

B-BUT WE MAY OVERTAKE THOSE MEN!

OH! NEVER MIND **THAT.** IF WE MAKE HASTE, WE SHALL PASS THEM BY PRESENTLY, AND I AM **DYING** TO SHOW YOU MY HAT.

THEREFORE, TO SHOW THE INDEPENDENCE OF MISS THORPE, THEY SET OUT IMMEDIATELY AS FAST AS THEY COULD IN PURSUIT OF THE TWO YOUNG MEN.

CATHERINE AND ISABELLA WERE PREVENTED CROSSING THE STREET BY THE SWIFT APPROACH OF A CARRIAGE.

GOOD HEAVENS! 'TIS *JAMES!*

DELIGHTFUL! MR. MORLAND AND MY BROTHER!

DEAR SISTER, MAY I PRESENT MY FRIEND, JOHN THORPE?

AT YOUR SERVICE, BEWITCHING LADY.

MOTHER WILL BE *SO* HAPPY TO KNOW YOU ARE HERE, JOHN. LET US GO TO HER AT *ONCE!*

ARE YOU FOND OF AN OPEN CARRIAGE, MISS MORLAND? I SHALL DRIVE YOU UP LANSDOWN HILL TOMORROW.

THANK YOU; BUT WILL NOT YOUR HORSE WANT REST?

REST! NOTHING RUINS HORSES SO MUCH AS REST!

I SHALL EXERCISE MINE AN AVERAGE OF *FOUR HOURS* EVERY DAY WHILE I AM HERE.

HOW *DELIGHTFUL* THAT WILL BE!

AND I *WILL* DRIVE YOU TOMORROW.

JOHN'S DISCOURSE NOW TURNED TO A SENTENCE OF PRAISE OR CONDEMNATION ON THE FACE OF EVERY WOMAN THEY MET. CATHERINE VENTURED TO VARY THE SUBJECT.

HAVE YOU EVER READ *UDOLPHO,* MR. THORPE?

UDOLPHO! OH LORD! NOT *I;* I NEVER READ NOVELS — THEY ARE THE *STUPIDEST* THINGS IN CREATION!

THIS BROUGHT THEM TO THE DOOR OF MRS. THORPE'S LODGINGS.

AH, MOTHER, WHERE *DID* YOU GET THAT QUIZ OF A HAT?

JOHN, YOU SILLY, *SILLY* BOY!

IT MAKES YOU LOOK LIKE AN OLD *WITCH!*

THESE MANNERS DID NOT PLEASE CATHERINE, BUT HE WAS JAMES'S FRIEND AND ISABELLA'S BROTHER.

JOHN ENGAGED HER BEFORE THEY PARTED TO DANCE WITH HIM THAT EVENING.

OH DEAR!

KATHUMP KATHUMP

DESPITE THORPE'S CRITIQUE, CATHERINE SPENT THE AFTERNOON IN THE LUXURY OF A RESTLESS AND FRIGHTENED IMAGINATION OVER THE PAGES OF *UDOLPHO.*

THAT EVENING, JAMES WAS VERY EAGER TO DANCE WITH ISABELLA, BUT JOHN HAD GONE INTO THE CARD-ROOM TO SPEAK WITH A FRIEND.

I *ASSURE* YOU, I WOULD NOT DESERT YOUR DEAR SISTER FOR ALL THE *WORLD!*

HMM...

CATHERINE ACCEPTED THIS KINDNESS WITH GRATITUDE, AND THEY CONTINUED AS THEY WERE FOR THREE MINUTES LONGER.

MY DEAR CREATURE, I AM AFRAID I *MUST* LEAVE YOU, YOUR BROTHER IS *SO* AMAZINGLY IMPATIENT TO BEGIN.

I *KNOW* YOU WILL NOT MIND MY GOING AWAY, AND I DARE SAY JOHN WILL BE BACK IN A MOMENT.

CATHERINE WAS LEFT TO THE MERCY OF MRS. THORPE AND MRS. ALLEN.

SHE WAS ROUSED, AT THE END OF TEN MINUTES, BY SEEING, NOT MR. THORPE, BUT MR. TILNEY, LOOKING AS HANDSOME AS EVER AND TALKING WITH A FASHIONABLE YOUNG WOMAN.

OH! I AM *SURE* THAT MUST BE HIS SISTER!

MISS MORLAND, I AM HAPPY TO SEE YOU. PRAY ALLOW ME TO INTRODUCE MY SISTER, ELEANOR.

I AM VERY HAPPY TO SEE YOU, INDEED; I WAS AFRAID YOU HAD LEFT BATH.

I *HAD* QUITTED IT FOR A WEEK, ON THE VERY MORNING AFTER HAVING HAD THE PLEASURE OF SEEING YOU.

SHE *IS* HIS SISTER!

MR. TILNEY HAD JUST ASKED CATHERINE TO DANCE, WHEN THORPE FINALLY RETURNED.

HEYDAY, MISS MORLAND! WHAT IS THE *MEANING* OF THIS? I THOUGHT *YOU AND I* WERE TO DANCE TOGETHER!

IT WAS WITH TERRIBLE REGRET THAT SHE GAVE HER DENIAL, DUE TO HER PRIOR COMMITMENT TO MR. THORPE.

I WAS SPEAKING WITH MY FRIEND WHO HAS GOT A HORSE TO SELL, A FAMOUS CLEVER ANIMAL FOR THE ROAD, ONLY *FORTY GUINEAS.*

I HAD FIFTY MINDS TO BUY IT *MYSELF,* FOR IT IS ONE OF MY MAXIMS *ALWAYS* TO BUY A GOOD HORSE WHEN I MEET WITH ONE...

BUT IT WOULD NOT ANSWER *MY* PURPOSE, IT WOULD NOT DO FOR THE *FIELD.*

I WOULD GIVE ANY MONEY FOR A REAL *GOOD* HUNTER. I HAVE *THREE* NOW — I WOULD NOT TAKE *EIGHT HUNDRED GUINEAS* FOR THEM.

THORPE AGAIN LEFT TO BARGAIN WITH HIS FRIEND, AND CATHERINE RETURNED TO THE TILNEYS.

CATHERINE WAS GREATLY INTERESTED IN MISS TILNEY, WHO SEEMED CAPABLE OF BEING YOUNG, ATTRACTIVE, AND AT A BALL WITHOUT WANTING TO FIX THE ATTENTION OF EVERY MAN NEAR HER.

CATHERINE WAS FURTHER DELIGHTED BY MR. TILNEY, WHO AGAIN SOLICITED HER TO DANCE.

AS THEY DANCED, CATHERINE PERCEIVED HERSELF TO BE EARNESTLY REGARDED BY A GENTLEMAN AMONG THE LOOKERS-ON.

I SEE YOU NOTICED THE GENTLEMAN IN THE CROWD. HE IS GENERAL TILNEY, MY FATHER.

BEFORE THE EVENING CONCLUDED, IT WAS PROPOSED BY THE BROTHER AND SISTER THAT THEY SHOULD JOIN IN A WALK.

DO NOT LET US PUT IT OFF! LET US GO *TOMORROW!*

A TWELVE O'CLOCK MEETING WAS READILY AGREED TO, WITH ONLY A PROVISO THAT IT DID NOT RAIN.

THE MORROW BROUGHT A VERY SOBER-LOOKING DAY, THE SUN MAKING ONLY A FEW EFFORTS TO APPEAR.

OH DEAR! I DO BELIEVE IT WILL BE *WET.*

I THOUGHT HOW IT WOULD BE.

OH! THAT WE HAD SUCH WEATHER HERE AS THEY HAD AT *UDOLPHO!*

AT ABOUT ELEVEN O'CLOCK, A FEW SPECKS OF RAIN UPON THE WINDOW CAUGHT CATHERINE'S WATCHFUL EYE.

AT HALF PAST TWELVE, THE SKY BEGAN TO CLEAR.

I ALWAYS THOUGHT IT WOULD CLEAR UP.

CATHERINE'S NOTICE WAS CLAIMED BY THE APPROACH OF TWO OPEN CARRIAGES. A MOMENT LATER, JOHN THORPE CAME RUNNING UPSTAIRS.

COME, MISS MORLAND, BE *QUICK,* FOR THE *OTHERS* ARE IN A CONFOUNDED HURRY TO BE OFF!

WHAT DO YOU *MEAN?* WHERE ARE YOU ALL GOING TO?

WHY, YOU HAVE NOT *FORGOTTEN* OUR *ENGAGEMENT!* DID WE NOT AGREE TO TAKE A DRIVE THIS MORNING?

I CANNOT GO WITH YOU TODAY, BECAUSE I EXPECT MISS TILNEY AND HER BROTHER TO CALL ON ME TO TAKE A COUNTRY WALK.

HMMM...

YOU ARE TALKING OF THE MAN YOU DANCED WITH LAST NIGHT?

YES...

I SAW HIM JUST THIS MOMENT, DRIVING UP THE LANSDOWN ROAD WITH A SMART-LOOKING GIRL.

IT IS VERY ODD! BUT I SUPPOSE THEY THOUGHT IT TOO WET FOR A WALK.

MY *DEAREST* CREATURE, YOU HAVE BEEN AT LEAST *THREE HOURS* GETTING READY!

MAKE HASTE AND GET IN, FOR I *LONG* TO BE OFF.

CATHERINE GAVE HERSELF UP TO THE ENJOYMENT OF THE FINE FEBRUARY AIR. A SILENCE OF SEVERAL MINUTES WAS BROKEN BY THORPE.

I SAY, OLD ALLEN IS *RICH*, IS HE NOT?

YES, I BELIEVE HE IS VERY RICH.

AND NO CHILDREN AT ALL?

NO — NOT ANY.

THEY PASSED BRISKLY DOWN PULTENEY STREET.

STOP, STOP, MR. THORPE, IT IS MISS TILNEY!

HOW *COULD* YOU TELL ME THEY WERE GONE?

STOP!

I WILL GET OUT *THIS MINUTE* AND GO TO THEM!

BUT THORPE ONLY LAUGHED, SMACKED HIS WHIP, AND DROVE ON.

HOW *COULD* YOU DECEIVE ME SO, MR. THORPE? THEY MUST THINK IT SO RUDE OF ME!

I DECLARE, I HAVE *NEVER* SEEN TWO MEN SO MUCH *ALIKE.*

THEY RETURNED TO PULTENEY STREET WITHOUT CATHERINE SPEAKING TWENTY WORDS.

AS THEY ENTERED THE HOUSE, MRS. ALLEN TOLD HER THE TILNEYS HAD CALLED A FEW MINUTES AFTER HER SETTING OFF.

THEY ALL SPENT THE EVENING TOGETHER AT THE THORPE'S.

IT WAS *AMAZINGLY* SHOCKING, TO BE SURE, BUT THE TILNEYS WERE *ENTIRELY* TO BLAME. WHY WERE THEY NOT MORE *PUNCTUAL*?

GOOD HEAVENS, WHAT A *DELIGHTFUL* HAND YOU HAVE GOT!

DEJECTED AND HUMBLED, CATHERINE HAD SOME THOUGHTS OF NOT GOING WITH MRS. ALLEN TO THE THEATER THE NEXT NIGHT, BUT IT WAS A PLAY SHE WANTED VERY MUCH TO SEE.

WHEN SHE OBSERVED HENRY TILNEY AND HIS FATHER IN THE OPPOSITE BOX, THE STAGE COULD NO LONGER KEEP HER ATTENTION.

THE PLAY CONCLUDED, AND HENRY TILNEY MADE HIS WAY TO THEIR BOX. HE GREETED CATHERINE AND MRS. ALLEN WITH A COOL POLITENESS.

OH! MR. TILNEY, YOU MUST HAVE THOUGHT ME SO *RUDE!*

BUT INDEED, IT WAS NOT MY OWN FAULT.

THEY TOLD ME THAT YOU AND YOUR SISTER HAD GONE OUT IN A CARRIAGE TOGETHER!

BUT WHEN I SAW YOU I *BEGGED* MR. THORPE TO STOP; AND, IF HE WOULD ONLY HAVE STOPPED, I WOULD HAVE JUMPED OUT AND RUN AFTER YOU!

BEFORE THEY PARTED, IT WAS AGREED THAT THEIR WALK WOULD BE TAKEN ON SUNDAY, AND CATHERINE WAS LEFT ONE OF THE HAPPIEST CREATURES IN THE WORLD.

CATHERINE'S OTHER FRIENDS, HOWEVER, HAD DIFFERENT IDEAS FOR SUNDAY.

DEAREST CREATURE, IT HAS BEEN *AGREED* THAT WE SHALL DRIVE TO CLIFTON ON SUNDAY.

I AM AFRAID IT IS IMPOSSIBLE FOR ME TO ACCOMPANY YOU.

I HAVE PROMISED MISS TILNEY TO TAKE OUR PROPOSED WALK ON SUNDAY.

IT WOULD BE SO *EASY* TO TELL MISS TILNEY THAT YOU HAD JUST BEEN REMINDED OF A *PRIOR* ENGAGEMENT, AND MUST PUT OFF THE WALK 'TIL TUESDAY.

NO, I COULD NOT DO THAT.

THEY CONTINUED WALKING, IN A MOST UNCOMFORTABLE MANNER.

PUFF PUFF PUFF

NO, NO, *NO!*

NAY, CATHERINE. I SHALL THINK YOU QUITE *UNKIND*, IF YOU STILL REFUSE.

WELL, *I* HAVE *SETTLED* THE MATTER. I HAVE BEEN TO MISS TILNEY, AND MADE YOUR EXCUSES.

YOU HAVE *NOT!*

I CAUGHT UP WITH HER ON HER WAY HOME, AND TOLD HER THAT YOU HAD SENT ME TO SAY THAT YOU COULD NOT HAVE THE PLEASURE OF WALKING WITH HER 'TIL TUESDAY. A PRETTY GOOD THOUGHT OF MINE — HEY?

THIS WILL NOT DO! I MUST RUN AFTER MISS TILNEY AND SET HER RIGHT!

THE TILNEYS WERE TURNING INTO THEIR LODGINGS AS CATHERINE CAME WITHIN VIEW OF THEIR HOUSE.

WHEEZE

IT WAS ALL A *MISTAKE* — I NEVER PROMISED TO GO!

I RAN ALL THE WAY TO *EXPLAIN!*

WHATEVER MIGHT HAVE BEEN FELT BEFORE HER ARRIVAL, HER EAGER DECLARATIONS IMMEDIATELY MADE AMENDS.

THE MORNING WAS FAIR, AND CATHERINE FEARED ANOTHER ATTACK FROM THE ASSEMBLED PARTY. SHE WAS HEARTILY REJOICED AT NEITHER SEEING NOT HEARING ANYTHING FROM THEM. THE TILNEYS DETERMINED ON WALKING ROUND BEECHEN CLIFF.

I NEVER LOOK AT IT WITHOUT THINKING OF THE SOUTH OF FRANCE.

YOU HAVE BEEN ABROAD THEN?

OH! NO, I ONLY MEAN WHAT I HAVE READ ABOUT...

IT ALWAYS PUTS ME IN MIND OF THE COUNTRY THAT EMILY AND HER FATHER TRAVELED THROUGH, IN *THE MYSTERIES OF UDOLPHO.*

BUT *YOU* NEVER READ NOVELS, I DARE SAY?

WHY NOT?

BECAUSE GENTLEMEN READ *BETTER* BOOKS.

THE PERSON WHO HAS NOT PLEASURE IN A GOOD NOVEL MUST BE *INTOLERABLY* STUPID.

I HAVE READ *ALL* MRS. RADCLIFFE'S WORK, AND *THE MYSTERIES OF UDOLPHO*, WHEN I HAD ONCE BEGUN IT, I COULD NOT LAY DOWN AGAIN.

I AM VERY GLAD TO HEAR IT, INDEED.

AND NOW I SHALL NEVER BE ASHAMED OF LIKING *UDOLPHO* MYSELF.

THE WHOLE WALK WAS DELIGHTFUL, AND IT ENDED TOO SOON.

EARLY THE NEXT DAY, A NOTE FROM ISABELLA HASTENED CATHERINE TO THE THORPE'S LODGINGS.

OH! MY DEAR CATHERINE, **YOU ALONE**, WHO KNOW MY HEART, CAN JUDGE OF MY PRESENT HAPPINESS. YOUR BROTHER IS THE MOST **CHARMING** OF MEN. I ONLY WISH I WERE MORE **WORTHY** OF HIM.

YES, MY **DEAR** CATHERINE; YOUR PENETRATION HAS NOT DECEIVED YOU.

OH! THAT **ARCH EYE** OF YOURS! IT SEES THROUGH **EVERYTHING**.

GOOD HEAVENS! MY DEAR ISABELLA — CAN YOU **REALLY** BE ENGAGED TO JAMES?

JAMES WAS PREPARING TO SET OFF WITH ALL SPEED, TO FULLERTON, TO ASK CONSENT.

I AM SURE MY FATHER AND MOTHER WOULD NEVER OPPOSE THEIR SON'S WISHES.

YET **DARE** I EXPECT IT? MY FORTUNE WILL BE **SO** SMALL — YOUR BROTHER, WHO MIGHT MARRY **ANYBODY**!

INDEED, ISABELLA, YOU ARE TOO HUMBLE. THE DIFFERENCE OF FORTUNE CAN BE NOTHING TO SIGNIFY.

AND WHEN THE LETTER ARRIVED, WHERE COULD BE DISTRESS BE FOUND?

HE WRITES: "I HAVE HAD NO DIFFICULTY IN GAINING THE CONSENT OF MY KIND PARENTS..."

"...AND AM PROMISED THAT EVERYTHING IN THEIR POWER SHALL BE DONE TO FORWARD MY HAPPINESS."

ISABELLA AND HER MOTHER RAN OFF TO ANNOUNCE THE CONTENTS OF THE LETTER, LEAVING JOHN IN THE PARLOR WITH CATHERINE.

A FAMOUS GOOD THING, THIS MARRYING SCHEME! I SAY IT IS NO BAD NOTION.

I AM SURE IT IS A VERY GOOD ONE.

DID YOU EVER HEAR THE OLD SONG "GOING TO ONE WEDDING BRINGS ON ANOTHER?"

I SAY, YOU KNOW, WE MAY TRY THE **TRUTH** OF THIS OLD SONG.

MAY WE? BUT I NEVER SING.

PRAY DO. MY FATHER AND MOTHER WILL BE VERY GLAD TO SEE YOU.

I SHALL COME AND PAY MY RESPECTS AT FULLERTON BEFORE LONG, IF NOT DISAGREEABLE.

AND I HOPE — I HOPE, MISS MORLAND, **YOU** WILL NOT BE SORRY TO SEE **ME**.

OH, DEAR! NOT AT ALL. THERE ARE VERY FEW PEOPLE I AM SORRY TO SEE. COMPANY IS ALWAYS CHEERFUL.

TOWARDS EVENING, CATHERINE JOINED ISABELLA ON THE UPPER ROOMS, WHERE SHE WAS INTRODUCED TO HENRY'S ELDER BROTHER, CAPTAIN TILNEY.

ISABELLA EXPRESSED HER RELUCTANCE TO DANCE.

OH, DO *NOT* INSIST ON MY BEING VERY AGREEABLE, FOR MY *HEART*, YOU KNOW, WILL BE SOME FORTY MILES OFF.

AND AS FOR *DANCING*, DO NOT *MENTION* IT; THAT IS *QUITE* OUT OF THE QUESTION.

DO YOU THINK YOUR FRIEND, MISS THORPE, WOULD HAVE ANY OBJECTION TO DANCING?

MY BROTHER WOULD BE MOST HAPPY TO BE INTRODUCED TO HER.

I AM *SURE* MISS THORPE DOES NOT MEAN TO DANCE AT ALL.

I SUPPOSE HE SAW ISABELLA SITTING DOWN, AND FANCIED SHE MIGHT WISH FOR A PARTNER...

...BUT HE IS QUITE MISTAKEN, FOR SHE HAS SAID SHE WOULD NOT DANCE UPON ANY ACCOUNT IN THE WORLD.

AND DID ISABELLA NEVER CHANGE HER MIND BEFORE?

WHY? WHAT DO YOU MEAN?

HENRY INDICATED THAT CATHERINE SHOULD LOOK BEHIND HER.

I CANNOT *THINK* HOW THAT COULD HAPPEN! ISABELLA WAS *SO* DETERMINED *NOT* TO DANCE!

WHEN THE YOUNG LADIES NEXT MET ON THE FOLLOWING DAY, JAMES'S SECOND LETTER WAS RECEIVED, AND THE FULL INTENTIONS OF HIS FATHER EXPLAINED.

A LIVING, OF ABOUT FOUR HUNDRED POUNDS YEARLY VALUE, IS TO BE RESIGNED BY MR. MORLAND TO JAMES...

HMPH

VERY CHARMING, INDEED.

IF MR. MORLAND FINDS HE CAN DO MORE BY AND BY, I DARE SAY HE WILL. I AM SURE HE *MUST* BE AN EXCELLENT, GOOD-HEARTED MAN.

IT IS NOT ON MY *OWN* ACCOUNT I WISH FOR MORE;

BUT I CAN HARDLY *BEAR* TO BE THE MEANS OF INJURING MY DEAR JAMES —

— MAKING HIM SIT DOWN UPON AN INCOME HARDLY ENOUGH TO FIND ONE IN THE COMMON *NECESSARIES* OF LIFE.

LATER THAT MORNING CATHERINE VISITED MISS TILNEY.

BUT PERHAPS — YOU WOULD BE SO GOOD — IT WOULD MAKE ME VERY HAPPY IF —

MY FATHER HAS DETERMINED UPON QUITTING BATH BY THE END OF ANOTHER WEEK.

WELL, ELEANOR, MAY I *CONGRATULATE* YOU ON BEING *SUCCESSFUL* IN YOUR APPLICATION TO YOUR FAIR FRIEND?

I WAS JUST BEGINNING TO MAKE THE REQUEST, SIR, AS YOU CAME IN.

MY DAUGHTER, MISS MORLAND, HAS BEEN FORMING A VERY BOLD WISH. CAN YOU BE PREVAILED UPON TO QUIT THIS SCENE OF PUBLIC TRIUMPH AND OBLIGE YOUR FRIEND ELEANOR WITH YOUR COMPANY IN GLOUCESTERSHIRE?

'TIS TRUE, WE CAN OFFER YOU NOTHING LIKE THE GAIETIES OF THIS LIVELY PLACE, YET NO ENDEAVORS SHALL BE WANTING ON OUR SIDE TO MAKE NORTHANGER ABBEY NOT WHOLLY DISAGREEABLE.

NORTHANGER ABBEY! THESE THRILLING WORDS COMPLETED CATHERINE'S CONVICTION OF BEING FAVORED BEYOND EVERY OTHER HUMAN CREATURE. SHE WAS TO BE FOR WEEKS UNDER THE SAME ROOF WITH THE PERSON WHOSE SOCIETY SHE MOST PRIZED — AND THIS ROOF WAS TO BE THE ROOF OF AN ABBEY!

WITH A MIND THUS FULL OF HAPPINESS, CATHERINE WAS HARDLY AWARE THAT THREE DAYS HAD PASSED WITHOUT HER SEEING ISABELLA.

BUT ONE MORNING AS SHE WALKED ALONG THE PUMP ROOM, ISABELLA APPEARED AND LED THE WAY TO A SEAT.

I HAVE JUST HAD A LETTER FROM JOHN; YOU CAN *GUESS* THE CONTENTS.

NO, INDEED, I CANNOT.

HE SAYS IN THIS LETTER THAT HE AS GOOD AS MADE YOU AN OFFER, AND THAT YOU RECEIVED HIS ADVANCES IN THE KINDEST WAY.

YOU *KNOW* HE IS OVER HEAD AND EARS IN *LOVE* WITH YOU.

PRAY UNDECEIVE HIM AS SOON AS YOU CAN! I CERTAINLY CANNOT RETURN HIS AFFECTION, AND AS CERTAINLY NEVER MEANT TO ENCOURAGE IT.

AH, WELL! A LITTLE HARMLESS FLIRTATION *WILL* OCCUR...

...AND ONE *IS* OFTEN DRAWN ON TO GIVE MORE ENCOURAGEMENT THAN ONE WISHES TO *STAND* BY.

CATHERINE OBSERVED THAT ISABELLA'S EYES WERE CONTINUALLY BENT TOWARDS THE DOOR, AS IN EAGER EXPECTATION.

BUT WHO *ARE* YOU LOOKING FOR?

I AM NOT LOOKING FOR ANYBODY. ONE'S EYES, YOU KNOW, *MUST* BE *SOMEWHERE*.

CATHERINE SUDDENLY PERCEIVED CAPTAIN TILNEY ENTER THROUGH THE DOOR. HE APPROACHED AND IMMEDIATELY TOOK THE SEAT NEXT TO ISABELLA.

HOW *FLATTERING* IT IS, ALWAYS TO BE WATCHED FOR.

PSHA, NONSENSE! MY *SPIRIT*, YOU KNOW, IS PRETTY INDEPENDENT.

I WISH YOUR *HEART* WERE INDEPENDENT AS WELL.

MY HEART, INDEED! YOU MEN HAVE *NONE* OF YOU ANY HEARTS.

IF WE HAVE NOT HEARTS, WE HAVE *EYES*; AND THEY GIVE US TORMENT ENOUGH.

DO THEY? I AM SORRY FOR IT; I AM SORRY THEY FIND *ANYTHING* SO DISAGREEABLE IN *ME*.

CATHERINE COULD LISTEN NO LONGER. SHE WALKED OUT OF THE PUMP ROOM, LEAVING ISABELLA STILL SITTING WITH CAPTAIN TILNEY.

THE BUSTLE OF LEAVING BATH WAS NOT PLEASANT. THE MAID HAD SO CROWDED THE CHAISE WITH PARCELS THAT THERE WAS LITTLE ROOM TO SIT. THEY SET OFF AT A SOBER PACE, THE GENERAL FOLLOWING IN HIS SON'S CARRIAGE.

CATHERINE'S SPIRITS REVIVED AFTER A SUPPER AT AN INN, WHEN THE GENERAL PROPOSED SHE TAKE HIS PLACE IN THE CARRIAGE FOR THE REST OF THE WAY.

THE DAY IS FINE, AND I WISH FOR YOU TO SEE AS MUCH OF THE COUNTRY AS POSSIBLE.

CATHERINE SEATED HERSELF WITH HENRY, AS HAPPY A BEING AS EVER EXISTED.

HAVE YOU FORMED A FAVORABLE IDEA OF THE ABBEY?

IS IT NOT A FINE OLD PLACE, JUST LIKE ONE READS ABOUT?

AND ARE YOU PREPARED TO ENCOUNTER ALL THE *HORRORS* THAT A BUILDING SUCH AS "ONE READS ABOUT" MAY PRODUCE? HAVE YOU A STOUT HEART? NERVES FIT FOR SLIDING PANELS AND SECRET DOORS?

BUT YOU *MUST* BE AWARE THAT WHEN A YOUNG LADY IS INTRODUCED TO A DWELLING OF THIS KIND, SHE IS *ALWAYS* LODGED APART FROM THE REST OF THE FAMILY. SHE IS CONDUCTED BY AN ANCIENT HOUSEKEEPER ALONG GLOOMY PASSAGES, INTO AN APARTMENT NEVER USED SINCE SOME KIN DIED IN IT TWENTY YEARS BEFORE.

THE HOUSEKEEPER GIVES YOU REASON TO SUPPOSE THAT THE ABBEY IS UNDOUBTEDLY *HAUNTED.* AND WHEN YOU ATTEMPT TO FASTEN YOUR DOOR, YOU DISCOVER THAT IT HAS NO LOCK.

ON THE THIRD NIGHT AFTER YOUR ARRIVAL, YOU WILL PROBABLY HAVE A *VIOLENT* STORM. YOU WILL DISCOVER A DIVISION IN A TAPESTRY SO ARTFULLY CONSTRUCTED AS TO DEFY INSPECTION, AND ON OPENING IT, A DOOR WILL IMMEDIATELY APPEAR — AND, WITH YOUR LAMP IN HAND, WILL PASS THROUGH INTO A SMALL ROOM.

OH! MR. TILNEY, HOW *FRIGHTFUL!* THIS IS JUST LIKE A BOOK! BUT WHAT *THEN?*

NO, INDEED: I SHOULD BE TOO MUCH *FRIGHTENED* TO DO *ANY* SUCH THING.

"YOU WILL PROCEED INTO THIS SMALL ROOM, AND THROUGH THIS INTO SEVERAL OTHERS, WITHOUT PERCEIVING ANYTHING REMARKABLE. IN ONE, PERHAPS A DAGGER, IN ANOTHER A FEW DROPS OF BLOOD, AND IN A THIRD THE REMAINS OF SOME INSTRUMENT OF TORTURE —"

"IN REPASSING THROUGH THE SMALL ROOM, YOUR EYES WILL BE ATTRACTED TOWARDS A LARGE, OLD-FASHIONED CABINET OF EBONY AND GOLD. YOU WILL SEARCH INTO EVERY DRAWER. AT LAST, BY TOUCHING A SECRET SPRING, AN INNER COMPARTMENT WILL OPEN — A ROLL OF PAPERS APPEARS..."

"...WHEN YOUR LAMP SUDDENLY EXPIRES, AND LEAVES YOU IN TOTAL DARKNESS."

"— BUT THERE BEING NOTHING IN ALL THIS OUT OF THE COMMON WAY, YOU WILL RETURN TOWARDS YOUR OWN APARTMENT."

OH! NO, NO — DO NOT SAY SO! WELL, GO ON.

HA HA HA!

AS THEY DREW NEAR THE END OF THEIR JOURNEY, EVERY BEND IN THE ROAD WAS EXPECTED TO AFFORD A GLIMPSE OF THE ABBEY'S MASSY WALLS OF GRAY STONE, RISING AMIDST A GROVE OF ANCIENT OAKS.

BUT SO LOW DID THE BUILDING STAND, THAT SHE FOUND HERSELF PASSING THROUGH THE GREAT GATES INTO THE VERY GROUNDS OF NORTHANGER, WITHOUT HAVING DISCERNED EVEN AN ANTIQUE CHIMNEY.

YES, IT WAS DELIGHTFUL TO BE REALLY IN AN ABBEY! THE FURNITURE WAS ELEGANT, AND OF MODERN TASTE. THE FIREPLACE HAD OVER IT ORNAMENTS OF THE PRETTIEST CHINA. THE WINDOWS WERE OF GOTHIC FORM, THE POINTED ARCHES PRESERVED WITH CARE —

— BUT EVERY PANE WAS SO CLEAR, SO LIGHT! TO AN IMAGINATION WHICH HAD HOPED FOR PAINTED GLASS AND COBWEBS, THE DIFFERENCE WAS VERY DISTRESSING.

HARRUMPH!

IT IS *TWENTY* MINUTES OF FIVE. DINNER IS TO BE ON THE TABLE *DIRECTLY!*

THE GENERAL'S TONE CONVINCED CATHERINE THAT STRICT PUNCTUALITY TO THE FAMILY HOURS WOULD BE EXPECTED AT NORTHANGER.

MISS TILNEY LED THE WAY UP A BROAD STAIRCASE OF SHINING OAK, ALONG A LONG, WIDE GALLERY, AND INTO A CHAMBER, AND LEFT HER WITH AN ANXIOUS ENTREATY THAT SHE WOULD HURRY WITH HER PREPARATIONS FOR DINNER.

A MOMENT'S GLANCE WAS ENOUGH TO SATISFY CATHERINE THAT HER APARTMENT CONTAINED NEITHER TAPESTRY NOR VELVET AND WAS ALTOGETHER FAR FROM UNCHEERFUL.

MISS TILNEY SOON ENTERED THE ROOM, AND HINTED HER FEAR OF BEING LATE.

THEY RAN DOWNSTAIRS TOGETHER, TO THE DRAWING ROOM.

PUFF PUFF

HARRUMPH!

THE DINING PARLOR WAS A NOBLE ROOM, FITTED UP IN A STYLE OF LUXURY WHICH WAS ALMOST LOST ON THE UNPRACTICED EYE OF CATHERINE, WHO SPOKE ALOUD HER ADMIRATION.

I *DO* LOOK UPON A TOLERABLY LARGE EATING-ROOM AS ONE OF THE *NECESSITIES* OF LIFE.

I SUPPOSE, HOWEVER, THAT YOU MUST BE USED TO MUCH *BETTER-SIZED* APARTMENTS AT MR. ALLEN'S?

NO INDEED. MR. ALLEN'S DINING PARLOR IS NOT MORE THAN *HALF* AS LARGE.

WELL, HARRUMPH, INDEED.

WITH THAT, THE GENERAL'S GOOD HUMOR INCREASED, AND THE EVENING PASSED WITHOUT ANY FURTHER DISTURBANCE.

THE NIGHT WAS STORMY, AND AS CATHERINE LISTENED TO THE TEMPEST WITH SENSATIONS OF AWE, SHE FELT FOR THE FIRST TIME THAT SHE WAS REALLY IN AN ANCIENT ABBEY.

CATHERINE WAS BEGINNING TO THINK OF GETTING INTO BED, WHEN SHE WAS STRUCK BY THE APPEARANCE OF A HIGH, OLD-FASHIONED CABINET WHICH HAD NOT CAUGHT HER NOTICE BEFORE.

HMMM...

SHE HAD A STRANGE FANCY TO LOOK INTO IT; NOT, HOWEVER, WITH THE SMALLEST EXPECTATION OF FINDING ANYTHING.

HER EYES FELL ON A ROLL OF PAPER PUSHED BACK INTO THE FARTHEST PART OF THE CAVITY.

CATHERINE'S HEART FLUTTERED, HER KNEES TREMBLED, AND HER CHEEKS GREW PALE.

KATHUMP KATHUMP

SHE SEIZED, WITH AN UNSTEADY HAND, THE PRECIOUS MANUSCRIPT, AND RESOLVED INSTANTLY TO PERUSE EVERY LINE.

EEEK!

ALAS! IN MOVING THE CANDLE, CATHERINE EXTINGUISHED IT!

GROPING HER WAY TO THE BED, SHE JUMPED HASTILY IN, CREEPING FAR UNDERNEATH THE CLOTHES.

THE STORM STILL RAGED, AND STRANGE NOISES STRUCK ON HER STARTLED EAR. HOUR AFTER HOUR PASSED BEFORE THE TEMPEST SUBSIDED, AND THE WEARIED CATHERINE FELL ASLEEP.

THE HOUSEMAID'S PULLING BACK THE DRAPES AT EIGHT O'CLOCK THE NEXT DAY WAS THE SOUND THAT FIRST ROUSED CATHERINE; AND SHE OPENED HER EYES ON OBJECTS OF CHEERFULNESS.

A BRIGHT MORNING HAD SUCCEEDED THE TEMPEST OF THE NIGHT.

SHE INSTANTLY RECALLED THE MANUSCRIPT.

COULD IT BE POSSIBLE, OR DID HER EYES PLAY TRICKS? SHE HELD A WASHING-BILL IN HER HAND!

SHIRTS, STOCKINGS, CRAVATS AND WAISTCOATS — AND A FARRIER'S BILL!

THIS WAS THE COLLECTION OF PAPERS WHICH HAD FILLED HER WITH SUCH EXPECTATION AND ALARM.

SHE FOUND HER WAY WITH ALL SPEED TO THE BREAKFAST PARLOR. HENRY WAS ALONE IN IT.

GOOD MORNING, MISS MORLAND. I HOPE YOU WERE UNDISTURBED BY THE TEMPEST.

HEH

ER, THE WIND DID KEEP ME AWAKE A LITTLE, BUT WE HAVE A CHARMING MORNING AFTER IT.

HEAVEN FORBID THAT HENRY TILNEY SHOULD EVER KNOW HER FOLLY!

AFTER BREAKFAST, HENRY LEFT FOR HIS PROPERTY AT WOODSTON, WHERE BUSINESS WOULD KEEP HIM TWO OR THREE DAYS. THE GENERAL NOW PROPOSED THAT CATHERINE BE SHOWN OVER THE HOUSE, AND OFFERED HIMSELF AS HER CONDUCTOR. THOUGH SHE HAD HOPED TO EXPLORE IT ACCOMPANIED ONLY BY HIS DAUGHTER, IT WAS A PROPOSAL SHE GLADLY ACCEPTED.

BUT PERHAPS IT MIGHT BE MORE AGREEABLE TO YOU TO FIRST VISIT THE GARDENS? *YES*, I CAN READ IN YOUR EYES A *JUDICIOUS* DESIRE OF MAKING USE OF THE PRESENT FAVORABLE WEATHER.

I SHALL FETCH MY HAT AND ATTEND YOU IN A MOMENT.

CATHERINE HAD BEEN ALREADY EIGHTEEN HOURS IN THE ABBEY, AND HAD SEEN ONLY A FEW OF ITS ROOMS, SO SHE WENT TO PUT ON HER BONNET IN DISCONTENT.

BUT *WHERE* ARE YOU GOING, ELEANOR? WHY DO YOU CHOOSE *THAT* COLD, DAMP PATH?

MISS MORLAND WILL GET *WET*.

THIS IS *SO* FAVORITE A WALK OF MINE, THAT I ALWAYS THINK OF IT AS THE *BEST* WAY.

THE GENERAL EXCUSED HIMSELF FROM ATTENDING THEM; AND CATHERINE WAS SHOCKED TO FIND HOW MUCH HER SPIRITS WERE RELIEVED BY THE SEPARATION.

I AM PARTICULARLY FOND OF THIS SPOT. IT WAS MY MOTHER'S FAVORITE WALK.

SIGH

CATHERINE HAD NEVER HEARD MRS. TILNEY MENTIONED IN THE FAMILY BEFORE, AND SHE WAITED WITH INTEREST FOR SOMETHING MORE.

I USED TO WALK HERE SO OFTEN WITH HER! I NEVER LOVED IT THEN, AS I HAVE LOVED IT SINCE. HER MEMORY ENDEARS IT NOW.

AND OUGHT IT NOT TO ENDEAR IT TO HER HUSBAND? YET THE GENERAL WOULD NOT ENTER IT!

I WAS ONLY THIRTEEN WHEN SHE DIED; AND I COULD NOT, THEN, KNOW WHAT A LOSS IT WAS.

HER *PICTURE*, I SUPPOSE, HANGS IN YOUR *FATHER'S* ROOM...?

NO; IT WAS INTENDED FOR THE DRAWING ROOM, BUT MY FATHER WAS DISSATISFIED WITH THE PAINTING.

IT NOW HANGS IN MY BEDCHAMBER.

HERE WAS *ANOTHER* PROOF — A PORTRAIT OF A DEPARTED WIFE, NOT VALUED BY THE HUSBAND! HE MUST HAVE BEEN *DREADFULLY* CRUEL TO HER!

THE END OF THE PATH BROUGHT THEM DIRECTLY UPON THE GENERAL; AND IN SPITE OF HER INDIGNATION, SHE FOUND HERSELF OBLIGED TO WALK WITH HIM. THE GENERAL PROPOSED TO ESCORT CATHERINE ON THE MUCH-DELAYED TOUR OF THE ABBEY.

THEY RETURNED TO THE HALL, AND ASCENDED THE CHIEF STAIRCASE, THE GENERAL POINTING OUT THE BEAUTY OF ITS WOOD AND THE ORNAMENTS OF RICH CARVING.

ELEANOR, **WHERE** ARE YOU GOING?

HAS NOT MISS MORLAND **ALREADY** SEEN ALL THAT CAN BE WORTH HER NOTICE?

HAVING GAINED THE TOP, THEY TURNED IN THE OPPOSITE DIRECTION FROM THE GALLERY IN WHICH CATHERINE'S ROOM LAY.

AND DO YOU NOT SUPPOSE YOUR FRIEND MIGHT BE GLAD OF SOME **REFRESHMENT** AFTER SO MUCH EXERCISE?

S-SORRY, FATHER.

I WAS GOING TO TAKE YOU INTO MY MOTHER'S ROOM — THE ROOM IN WHICH SHE DIED.

IT WAS NO WONDER THAT THE GENERAL SHOULD SHRINK FROM THE SIGHT OF SUCH OBJECTS AS THAT ROOM MUST CONTAIN; A ROOM IN ALL PROBABILITY NEVER ENTERED BY HIM SINCE THE DREADFUL SCENE HAD PASSED WHICH RELEASED HIS SUFFERING WIFE.

SHE VENTURED, WHEN NEXT ALONE WITH ELEANOR, TO EXPRESS HER WISH OF BEING PERMITTED TO SEE THAT SIDE OF THE HOUSE.

IT REMAINS AS IT WAS, I SUPPOSE?

YES, ENTIRELY.

AND WERE YOU WITH YOUR MOTHER, TO THE LAST?

NO, I WAS UNFORTUNATELY FROM HOME. HER ILLNESS WAS SUDDEN AND SHORT; AND, BEFORE I ARRIVED IT WAS ALL OVER.

CATHERINE'S BLOOD RAN COLD WITH THE HORRID SUGGESTIONS THAT SPRANG FROM THESE WORDS. **COULD IT BE POSSIBLE—?**

THAT EVENING, CATHERINE WAS HEARTILY GLAD TO BE DISMISSED. THE GENERAL, HOWEVER, WAS NOT GOING TO RETIRE.

I HAVE MANY PAPERS TO FINISH BEFORE I CAN CLOSE *MY* EYES.

I *MAY*, PERHAPS, BE PORING OVER THE AFFAIRS OF THE NATION FOR *HOURS* AFTER YOU ARE ASLEEP.

BUT THE BUSINESS ALLEGED COULD NOT WIN CATHERINE FROM THINKING THAT A VERY *DIFFERENT* OBJECT MUST OCCASION SO SERIOUS A DELAY OF PROPER REPOSE.

THE PROBABILITY THAT MRS. TILNEY STILL *LIVED*, SHUT UP FOR CAUSES UNKNOWN, AND RECEIVING FROM THE PITILESS HANDS OF HER HUSBAND A NIGHTLY SUPPLY OF COARSE FOOD, WAS THE CONCLUSION WHICH *NECESSARILY* FOLLOWED.

THE NEXT MORNING, AS THE GENERAL TOOK HIS EARLY WALK, ELEANOR WAS READY TO OBLIGE HER REQUEST.

ELEANOR!!!

OH, DEAR!

CATHERINE RAN FOR SAFETY TO HER OWN ROOM...

...AND, LOCKING HERSELF IN, BELIEVED SHE SHOULD NEVER HAVE THE COURAGE TO GO DOWN AGAIN.

WHEW!

SHE REMAINED THERE AT LEAST AN HOUR, IN THE GREATEST AGITATION.

CATHERINE CAME TO THE RESOLUTION OF MAKING HER NEXT ATTEMPT ON THE FORBIDDEN DOOR ALONE. AT FOUR O'CLOCK SHE RETIRED TO DRESS HALF AN HOUR EARLIER THAN USUAL.

THE DOOR YIELDED TO HER HAND, AND ON TIPTOE SHE ENTERED.

BUT THIS APARTMENT, TO WHICH SHE HAD GIVEN A DATE SO ANCIENT, A POSITION SO AWFUL, PROVED TO BE DISTRESSINGLY PLEASANT!

ASTONISHMENT AND DOUBT SEIZED HER EMOTIONS, AND A SUCCEEDING RAY OF COMMON SENSE ADDED SOME BITTER EMOTIONS OF SHAME.

CLOMP CLOMP CLOMP

SHE WAS ON THE POINT OF RETREATING WHEN THE SOUND OF FOOTSTEPS MADE HER PAUSE AND TREMBLE.

MR. TILNEY! WHEN DID YOU RETURN?

HOW CAME YOU TO BE HERE?

I CAME UP THIS STAIRCASE BECAUSE IT IS THE SHORTEST WAY FROM THE STABLES TO MY OWN CHAMBER.

AND MAY I NOT, IN MY TURN, ASK HOW YOU CAME TO BE HERE?

I HAVE... BEEN TO SEE YOUR MOTHER'S ROOM.

MY MOTHER'S ROOM! IS THERE ANYTHING EXTRAORDINARY TO BE SEEN THERE?

NO... NOTHING AT ALL.

THIS MUST HAVE PROCEEDED FROM A SENTIMENT OF RESPECT FOR MY MOTHER'S CHARACTER, AS DESCRIBED BY ELEANOR. SHE HAS, I SUPPOSE, TALKED ABOUT HER A GREAT DEAL?

NO, NOT MUCH, BUT WITH HER DYING SO SUDDENLY, AND YOU — NONE OF YOU BEING AT HOME — AND YOUR FATHER, I THOUGHT — PERHAPS HAD NOT BEEN...FOND OF HER...

THE SEIZURE WHICH ENDED IN MY MOTHER'S DEATH *WAS* SUDDEN. THE MALADY ITSELF, A BILIOUS FEVER, WAS ONE FROM WHICH SHE HAD *OFTEN* SUFFERED.

A PHYSICIAN REMAINED IN ALMOST *CONSTANT* ATTENDANCE. I SAW HER *REPEATEDLY*, AND CAN BEAR WITNESS TO HER HAVING RECEIVED *EVERY POSSIBLE* ATTENTION.

IF I UNDERSTAND YOU *RIGHTLY*, YOU HAD FORMED A SURMISE OF SUCH *HORROR* AS I HAVE HARDLY *WORDS* TO —

DEAR MISS MORLAND, CONSIDER THE DREADFUL NATURE OF THE SUSPICIONS YOU HAVE ENTERTAINED!

CATHERINE WAS COMPLETELY HUMBLED.

SOB

WITH TEARS OF SHAME SHE RAN OFF TO HER ROOM.

CATHERINE'S FOLLY WAS EXPOSED, AND HE MUST DESPISE HER FOREVER. COULD HE *EVER* FORGIVE IT?

BUT AS THE EVENING WORE AWAY, HER SPIRITS WERE GRADUALLY RAISED TO A MODEST TRANQUILITY. SHE LEARNED TO HOPE THAT SHE HAD NOT LOST HENRY'S *ENTIRE* REGARD.

THE NEXT MORNING, WHEN CATHERINE ENTERED THE BREAKFAST ROOM, HER FIRST OBJECT WAS A LETTER HELD OUT BY HENRY'S WILLING HAND.

WHY, 'TIS FROM JAMES.

DEAR CATHERINE,
THOUGH, GOD KNOWS, WITH LITTLE INCLINATION FOR WRITING, I THINK IT MY DUTY TO TELL YOU THAT EVERYTHING IS AT AN END BETWEEN MISS THORPE AND ME. I LEFT HER AND BATH YESTERDAY, NEVER TO SEE EITHER AGAIN. I WISH YOUR VISIT AT NORTHANGER MAY BE OVER BEFORE CAPTAIN TILNEY MAKES HIS ENGAGEMENT KNOWN, OR YOU WILL BE UNCOMFORTABLY CIRCUMSTANCED. HER DUPLICITY HURTS ME MORE THAN ALL—; UNTIL THE VERY LAST SHE DECLARED HERSELF AS MUCH ATTACHED TO ME AS EVER.

NO BAD NEWS FROM FULLERTON, I HOPE?

NO, MY LETTER WAS FROM JAMES, AT OXFORD. I HAVE ONE FAVOR TO BEG:

THAT IF YOUR BROTHER SHOULD BE COMING HERE, YOU WILL GIVE ME NOTICE OF IT, THAT I MAY GO AWAY.

ISABELLA HAS DESERTED *MY* BROTHER, AND IS TO MARRY *YOURS.*

IF IT BE SO, I CAN ONLY SAY THAT FREDERICK WILL NOT BE THE FIRST MAN WHO HAS CHOSEN A WIFE WITH LESS SENSE THAN HIS FAMILY EXPECTED.

I DO *NOT* ENVY HIS SITUATION, EITHER AS A LOVER *OR* A SON.

BUT PERHAPS, THOUGH SHE HAS BEHAVED SO ILL BY OUR FAMILY, SHE MAY BEHAVE BETTER BY YOURS. NOW SHE HAS REALLY GOT THE MAN SHE LIKES, SHE MAY BE CONSTANT.

INDEED I AM AFRAID SHE WILL, UNLESS A *BARONET* SHOULD COME IN HER WAY.

THE MORNING AFTER THAT BROUGHT A VERY UNEXPECTED LETTER.

FROM ISABELLA?

THANK GOD WE LEAVE THIS VILE PLACE TOMORROW. SINCE YOU WENT AWAY, I HAVE HAD NO PLEASURE IN IT. I AM QUITE UNEASY ABOUT YOUR DEAR BROTHER, NOT HAVING HEARD FROM HIM SINCE HE WENT TO OXFORD; AND AM FEARFUL OF SOME MISUNDERSTANDING. IT IS VERY DIFFICULT TO KNOW WHOM TO TRUST, AND YOUNG MEN NEVER KNOW THEIR MINDS TWO DAYS TOGETHER. I REJOICE TO SAY THAT THE YOUNG MAN WHOM, OF ALL OTHERS, I PARTICULARLY ABHOR, HAS LEFT BATH.

YOU WILL KNOW, FROM THIS DESCRIPTION, I MUST MEAN CAPTAIN TILNEY. MANY GIRLS MIGHT HAVE BEEN TAKEN IN, BUT I KNEW THE FICKLE SEX TOO WELL. PRAY SEND ME SOME NEWS OF YOUR BROTHER — I AM AFRAID HE TOOK SOMETHING IN MY CONDUCT AMISS.

SO MUCH FOR ISABELLA! I DO NOT BELIEVE SHE HAD EVER ANY REGARD EITHER FOR JAMES OR ME, AND I WISH I HAD NEVER KNOWN HER!

SOON AFTER THIS, THE GENERAL FOUND HIMSELF OBLIGED TO GO TO LONDON FOR A WEEK. THE HAPPINESS WITH WHICH THEIR TIME NOW PASSED MADE CATHERINE THOROUGHLY SENSIBLE OF THE RESTRAINT WHICH THE GENERAL'S PRESENCE HAD IMPOSED, AND MOST THANKFULLY FEEL THEIR PRESENT RELEASE FROM IT.

HENRY WAS NOT ABLE TO REMAIN WHOLLY AT NORTHANGER IN ATTENDANCE ON THE LADIES; HIS ENGAGEMENTS AT WOODSTON OBLIGING HIM TO LEAVE THEM ON SATURDAY FOR A COUPLE OF NIGHTS.

THE TWO GIRLS FOUND THEMSELVES SO WELL SUFFICIENT FOR THE TIME TO THEMSELVES THAT SOON IT WAS ELEVEN O'CLOCK, RATHER A LATE HOUR AT THE ABBEY.

SUDDENLY A CARRIAGE WAS HEARD DRIVING UP TO THE DOOR.

I AM **SURE** THAT MUST BE MY BROTHER, FREDERICK, WHO OFTEN ARRIVES THIS SUDDENLY.

CATHERINE WALKED UP TO HER CHAMBER, MAKING UP HER MIND AS WELL AS SHE COULD, TO A FURTHER ACQUAINTANCE WITH CAPTAIN TILNEY.

I TRUST HE WILL NEVER SPEAK OF MISS THORPE; INDEED, HE **MUST**, BY THIS TIME, BE ASHAMED OF THE PART HE ACTED.

CATHERINE HEARD A HESITANT STEP IN THE GALLERY, AND SHE OPENED THE DOOR.

HOW SHALL I TELL YOU! OH! **HOW** SHALL I TELL YOU!

ERRAND! TO ME?

MY DEAR CATHERINE, YOU MUST NOT — YOU MUST NOT — INDEED, I CANNOT **BEAR** IT — I COME TO YOU ON **SUCH** AN ERRAND!

OH, NO! 'TIS A MESSENGER FROM **WOODSTON**!

IT IS NO MESSENGER FROM WOODSTON. IT IS MY FATHER HIMSELF. MY DEAR CATHERINE, WE ARE TO PART. MY FATHER HAS RECOLLECTED AN ENGAGEMENT WHICH TAKES OUR WHOLE FAMILY AWAY ON MONDAY.

AND I NEED NOT GO 'TIL JUST BEFORE *YOU* DO, YOU KNOW. DO NOT BE DISTRESSED, ELEANOR. THE GENERAL WILL SEND A SERVANT WITH ME, I DARE SAY, HALF THE WAY.

AH, CATHERINE! HOW CAN I TELL YOU? *TOMORROW MORNING* IS FIXED FOR YOUR LEAVING US. THE CARRIAGE IS ORDERED, AND WILL BE HERE AT SEVEN O'CLOCK...

...AND *NO* SERVANT WILL BE OFFERED YOU.

H-HAVE I *OFFENDED* THE GENERAL?

MY DEAR ELEANOR, DO NOT BE SO DISTRESSED. I AM VERY, VERY SORRY WE ARE TO PART; BUT I AM NOT OFFENDED, INDEED I AM NOT. I HOPE YOU WILL COME TO VISIT ME AT FULLERTON?

ALAS! FOR ALL THAT I KNOW, YOU HAVE GIVEN HIM NO JUST CAUSE FOR OFFENSE, BUT *SOMETHING* HAS OCCURRED TO RUFFLE HIS TEMPER IN AN *UNCOMMON* DEGREE.

IN ELEANOR'S PRESENCE FRIENDSHIP AND PRIDE HAD EQUALLY RESTRAINED HER TEARS, BUT NO SOONER WAS SHE GONE THAN THEY BURST FORTH IN TORRENTS!

OH, HENRY! WHO CAN SAY WHEN WE MIGHT MEET AGAIN?

SOB

TURNED FROM THE HOUSE, AND IN SUCH A WAY! WITHOUT ANY REASON THAT COULD JUSTIFY AND WITH HENRY AT A DISTANCE — NOT ABLE EVEN TO BID HIM FAREWELL!

THE CARRIAGE WAS READY AT SEVEN THE NEXT MORNING.

YOU MUST WRITE TO ME, CATHERINE. 'TIL I KNOW YOU TO BE SAFE AT HOME, I SHALL NOT HAVE AN HOUR'S COMFORT.

OH, ELEANOR, I WILL WRITE TO YOU, INDEED.

AND PLEASE CONVEY MY KIND REMEMBRANCE TO YOUR B-BROTHER, HEN — HENR —

BUT WITH THIS APPROACH TO HENRY'S NAME ENDED ALL POSSIBILITY OF RESTRAINING HER FEELINGS.

SOB
SOB

SNIFF

WHAT HAD SHE DONE, OR WHAT HAD SHE OMITTED TO DO, TO MERIT SUCH A CHANGE IN THE GENERAL?

BETWEEN SIX OR SEVEN O'CLOCK IN THE EVENING SHE FOUND HERSELF ENTERING FULLERTON.

A HEROINE RETURNING TO HER NATIVE VILLAGE IN SOLITUDE AND DISGRACE IN A HACK POST-CHAISE IS A DEPRESSING BLOW UPON SENTIMENT.

BUT, WHATEVER MIGHT BE THE DISTRESS OF CATHERINE'S MIND, HER RETURN WAS A PLEASURE QUITE UNLOOKED FOR BY HER FAMILY.

RELUCTANTLY, AND WITH MUCH HESITATION, DID CATHERINE BEGIN WHAT MIGHT PERHAPS BE TERMED AN EXPLANATION.

HMPH

SNIFF

I AM SORRY FOR THE YOUNG PEOPLE; THEY MUST HAVE A SAD TIME OF IT. BUT IT IS NO MATTER NOW; CATHERINE IS SAFE AT HOME, AND OUR COMFORT DOES *NOT* DEPEND UPON GENERAL TILNEY.

THOUGH, NEXT MORNING, CATHERINE'S RECOVERY WAS NOT EQUAL TO HER PARENTS' HOPES, THEY WERE STILL UNSUSPICIOUS OF THERE BEING ANY DEEPER EVIL — THEY NEVER ONCE THOUGHT ABOUT HER HEART!

CATHERINE COULD NEITHER SIT STILL, NOR EMPLOY HERSELF FOR TEN MINUTES TOGETHER, INSTEAD WALKING ROUND THE GARDEN AND ORCHARD AGAIN AND AGAIN.

BY NOW HENRY MUST HAVE ARRIVED AT NORTHANGER;

NOW HE MUST HAVE HEARD OF MY DEPARTURE;

AND NOW, PERHAPS, THEY ARE ALL SETTING OFF FOR HEREFORD.

MY DEAR CATHERINE, YOUR HEAD RUNS TOO MUCH UPON BATH; BUT THERE IS A TIME FOR *EVERYTHING* — A TIME FOR BALLS AND PLAYS, AND A TIME FOR *WORK*.

MY HEAD DOES NOT RUN UPON BATH... MUCH.

THEN YOU ARE FRETTING ABOUT GENERAL TILNEY, AND THAT IS VERY SIMPLE OF YOU; FOR TEN TO ONE WHETHER YOU EVER SEE HIM AGAIN. YOU SHOULD *NEVER* FRET ABOUT TRIFLES.

CATHERINE SAID NO MORE, AND WITH AN EFFORT TO DO RIGHT, APPLIED TO HER NEEDLEWORK WHILE HER MOTHER LEFT ON AN ERRAND.

LESS THAN AN HOUR HAD ELAPSED ERE MRS. MORLAND RETURNED AND BEHELD A YOUNG MAN WHOM SHE HAD NEVER SEEN BEFORE.

OH!

OH?

M-MOTHER, THIS IS HENRY TILNEY.

MADAME, I APOLOGIZE FOR MY APPEARANCE HERE. AFTER WHAT HAS PASSED, I HAVE LITTLE RIGHT TO EXPECT A WELCOME AT FULLERTON.

BUT I WAS IMPATIENT TO BE ASSURED OF MISS MORLAND'S HAVING REACHED HER HOME IN SAFETY.

PLEASE, SAY NOT ANOTHER WORD OF THE PAST. FRIENDS OF MY CHILDREN ARE ALWAYS WELCOME HERE.

MRS. MORLAND, THINKING IT PROBABLE THAT HE MIGHT HAVE SOME EXPLANATION TO COMMUNICATE ONLY TO CATHERINE, WOULD NOT ON ANY ACCOUNT PREVENT HER ACCOMPANYING HIM.

THEY BEGAN THEIR WALK; AND MRS. MORLAND WAS NOT ENTIRELY MISTAKEN IN HIS OBJECT IN WISHING IT.

ARE MR. AND MRS. ALLEN NOW AT FULLERTON? I SHOULD LIKE TO PAY MY RESPECTS TO THEM — IF YOU WILL BE SO KIND AS TO SHOW ME THE WAY?

BEFORE THEY REACHED MR. ALLEN'S GROUNDS, CATHERINE WAS ASSURED OF HIS AFFECTION; AND THAT HEART IN RETURN WAS SOLICITED, WHICH, PERHAPS, THEY PRETTY EQUALLY KNEW WAS ALREADY HIS OWN.

ON HIS RETURN FROM WOODSTON, TWO DAYS BEFORE, HENRY HAD BEEN MET BY HIS IMPATIENT FATHER, INFORMED IN ANGRY TERMS OF MISS MORLAND'S DEPARTURE, AND ORDERED TO THINK OF HER NO MORE.

UNDER A MISTAKEN PERSUASION OF HER POSSESSIONS AND CLAIMS, HE HAD DESIGNED HER FOR HIS DAUGHTER-IN-LAW.

THE GENERAL HAD HAD NOTHING TO ACCUSE HER OF. SHE WAS GUILTY ONLY OF BEING LESS RICH THAN HE HAD SUPPOSED HER TO BE.

JOHN THORPE HAD MISLED HIM. BEING AT THE TIME RESOLVED UPON MARRYING CATHERINE HIMSELF, HE REPRESENTED THE FAMILY AS YET MORE WEALTHY THAN HIS VANITY AND AVARICE HAD MADE HIM BELIEVE.

THAT ALL THIS WAS FALSE, THE GENERAL HAD LEARNED FROM THORPE HIMSELF, WHOM HE HAD CHANCED TO MEET IN TOWN, AND WHO, IRRITATED BY CATHERINE'S REFUSAL, CONFESSED HIMSELF TO HAVE BEEN TOTALLY MISTAKEN IN HIS OPINION OF CATHERINE'S CIRCUMSTANCE AND CHARACTER.

HE SAID HER FAMILY WERE, IN FACT, NECESSITOUS, AND SEEKING TO BETTER THEMSELVES BY WEALTHY CONNECTIONS.

THE GENERAL NEEDED NO MORE. ENRAGED, HE SET OUT THE NEXT DAY FOR THE ABBEY, WHERE HIS PERFORMANCE HAS BEEN SEEN.

HENRY'S INDIGNATION ON HEARING HOW CATHERINE HAD BEEN TREATED HAD BEEN OPEN AND BOLD.

THE GENERAL WAS FURIOUS IN HIS ANGER, AND THEY PARTED IN DREADFUL DISAGREEMENT.

MR. AND MRS. MORLAND'S SURPRISE ON BEING APPLIED TO BY MR. TILNEY FOR THEIR CONSENT TO HIS MARRYING THEIR DAUGHTER WAS CONSIDERABLE.

YOUR PLEASING MANNERS AND GOOD SENSE ARE SELF-EVIDENT RECOMMENDATIONS.

AND HAVING NEVER HEARD EVIL OF YOU, IT IS NOT *OUR* WAY TO SUPPOSE THAT EVIL CAN BE TOLD.

BUT I FEAR THAT CATHERINE WILL MAKE A SAD, HEEDLESS HOUSEKEEPER.

BUT THEY HAD NOT A SINGLE OBJECTION.

MADAM, THERE IS NOTHING LIKE PRACTICE.

THERE WAS BUT ONE OBSTACLE: UNTIL THE GENERAL'S CONSENT WAS GIVEN, IT WAS IMPOSSIBLE FOR THE MORLANDS TO SANCTION THE ENGAGEMENT.

...SO HENRY RETURNED TO HIS PROPERTY IN WOODSTON, AND CATHERINE REMAINED IN FULLERTON TO CRY.

BUT WHAT PROBABLE CIRCUMSTANCE COULD WORK UPON A TEMPER LIKE THE GENERAL'S TO AFFECT THE EARLY MARRIAGE OF HENRY AND CATHERINE?

THE CIRCUMSTANCE WHICH CHIEFLY AVAILED TOOK PLACE IN THE COURSE OF THE SUMMER...

... THE MARRIAGE OF HIS DAUGHTER WITH A MAN OF FORTUNE AND CONSEQUENCE — AN ACCESSION OF DIGNITY THAT THREW HIM INTO A FIT OF GOOD HUMOR.

FATHER, FOR MY WEDDING PRESENT, WON'T YOU FORGIVE HENRY?

VERY WELL, YOU HAVE MY PERMISSION TO BE A FOOL IF YOU LIKE IT.

AS SOON AS THE GENERAL WOULD ALLOW HIMSELF TO BE INFORMED, HE FOUND THAT HE HAD BEEN SCARCELY MORE MISLED BY THORPE'S FIRST BOAST OF THE MORLAND'S WEALTH THAN BY HIS SUBSEQUENT MALICIOUS OVERTHROW OF IT...

MORE TEA, GENERAL?

HARRUMPH! THANK YOU.

... AND THAT IN NO SENSE OF THE WORD WERE THEY NECESSITOUS OR POOR.

THE AWAITED EVENT SOON FOLLOWED; THE BELLS RANG, AND HENRY AND CATHERINE WERE MARRIED.

To BEGIN PERFECT HAPPINESS AT THE RESPECTIVE AGES OF TWENTY-SIX AND EIGHTEEN IS TO DO PRETTY WELL; AND PROFESSING MYSELF MOREOVER CONVINCED THAT THE GENERAL'S UNJUST INTERFERENCE, SO FAR FROM BEING REALLY INJURIOUS TO THEIR FELICITY, WAS PERHAPS RATHER CONDUCTIVE TO IT, BY IMPROVING THEIR KNOWLEDGE OF EACH OTHER AND ADDING STRENGTH TO THEIR ATTACHMENT, I LEAVE IT TO BE SETTLED, BY WHOMSOEVER IT MAY CONCERN, WHETHER THE TENDENCY OF THIS WORK BE ALTOGETHER TO RECOMMEND PARENTAL TYRANNY, OR REWARD FILIAL DISOBEDIENCE.

— JANE AUSTEN, 1803

AT THE GATE

by Myla Jo Closser

adapted by
Tom Pomplun

illustrated by
Shary Flenniken

A shaggy Airedale scented his way along the road. He had not been there before, but he was guided by the trail of his brethren who had preceded him. The path had been lonely, but the traces of countless dogs before him promised companionship at the end of the road.

The translation from recent agony into freedom from pain had been so numbing in its swiftness that it was some time before he could fully appreciate the pleasant country through which he was passing.

There were woods with leaves upon the ground through which to scurry, long grassy slopes for extended runs, and lakes into which he might plunge for sticks and bring them back to — But he did not complete his thought, as a little wave of homesickness possessed him.

It made his mind easier to see far ahead a great gate as high as the heavens, through which he fancied he could discern humans passing to whatever lay beyond.

The scent of the dogs grew very strong now, and coming nearer, he discovered, to his astonishment, that thousands of dogs were gathered on the outside of the portal.

They sat spread out on each side of the entrance; dogs of every age and variety.

All were apparently waiting for something, and at the pad of the Airedale's feet on the hard road they arose and looked in his direction.

That the interest passed as soon as they discovered the newcomer to be a dog puzzled him. In his former dwelling-place a four-footed brother was greeted with enthusiasm when he was a friend, or with sharp reproof when an enemy; but never had he been utterly ignored.

He remembered something that he had read many times on great buildings with lofty entrances, and he feared this might be the reason for the crowd outside the gate.

As he advanced cautiously to examine the gate, despair entered his soul. What bitter punishment these poor beasts must have suffered before they learned to stay on this side of an arch that led to human beings!

What had they done on earth to merit this? Stolen bones troubled his conscience, runaway days, and sleeping in the best chair until the key clicked in the lock.

As he reflected on past sins, a stranger approached him, snuffling in a friendly way.

I *KNOW* YOU! WHAT'S YOUR NAME?

TAM O'SHANTER. MY PEOPLE CALL ME TAMMY.

YES, BUT—

BUT WHAT?

WHAT OF THE DOGS THAT DON'T *HAVE* ANY PEOPLE?

OH, *EVERYTHING* IS THOUGHT OUT HERE. LAY DOWN, AND WATCH.

Soon they spied another small form making his way up the road. He wore a Boy Scout's uniform and was a little fearful, so new was this adventure. A pack of odds and ends of the company ran down to meet him.

THEY DIDN'T *KNOW* EACH OTHER!

THAT'S ONE OF THE CHILDREN WHO USED TO *BEG* FOR A DOG, BUT HIS FATHER WOULDN'T LET HIM HAVE ONE.

ALL OUR STRAYS WAIT FOR JUST SUCH LITTLE FELLOWS TO COME ALONG.

EVERY CHILD GETS A DOG, AND EVERY DOG GETS A MASTER!

LISA K. WEBER (*front cover, page 4*)

Lisa is a graduate of Parsons School of Design in New York City, where she is currently employed in the fashion industry, designing prints and characters for teenage girls' jammies, while freelancing work on children's books and character design for animation. Other projects include her "creaturized" opera posters and playing cards. Lisa has provided illustrations for *Graphic Classics: Edgar Allan Poe, Graphic Classics: H.P. Lovecraft, Graphic Classics: Ambrose Bierce, Graphic Classics: Bram Stoker* and *Graphic Classics: Mark Twain*, and adapted *The Gift of the Magi* in *Graphic Classics: O. Henry*. Illustrations excerpted from her in-progress book *The Shakespearean ABCs* were printed in *Rosebud 25*. More of Lisa's work can be seen online at www.creatureco.com.

CARLO VERGARA (*page 1, 44*)

Carlo Vergara is a comics creator living in the Philippines. His gay superhero graphic novel *Zsazsa Zaturnnah* won a National Book Award from the Manila Critics Circle, its musical adaptation has run onstage and the story has recently been optioned for a film. Carlo started writing his own comics professionally in 2001 with the drama *One Night In Purgatory*, though he has been drawing comics since 1993. A graphic designer by profession, he has spent most of his career in public relations and marketing communications, and has also dabbled in acting for theater and teaching in the university classroom. His comics adaptation of *Captain Blood* for *Graphic Classics: Rafael Sabatini* was Carlo's first work to be published in the U.S.

JANE AUSTEN (*page 2, 94*)

Jane Austen was born in rural England in 1775, the seventh of eight children of the Reverend George Austen and his wife, Cassandra. She was educated mainly at home and never lived apart from her family until her death from Addison's Disease at age forty-one. None of the books published in her lifetime had her name on them — they were credited as "By a Lady," though her name and stories are famous today, and numerous films have been adapted from her novels. *Northanger Abbey*, a satire of the then-popular gothic romance, and especially of *The Mysteries of Udolpho*, was sold to a publisher in 1803, but was not printed until 1818, a year after her death. She is regarded as one of the great masters of the English novel, though she also wrote occasional humorous verse, as evidenced by *I've a Pain in my Head*.

MOLLY KIELY (*page 2*)

Molly Kiely is a Canadian artist best known for her *Diary of a Dominatrix* comics series and the graphic novels *That Kind of Girl* and *Tecopa Jane*, all published by Fantagraphics. One of her portraits of Marilyn Monroe was recently reproduced in the updated edition of *Marilyn in Art*. Molly currently lives in Tucson, Arizona with her husband. She gave birth to their first child, a daughter, in March 2007. She is now working on an adaptation of *Salome* for *Graphic Classics: Oscar Wilde*. Molly can be reached via her website, www.mollykiely.com.

ANNE TIMMONS (*page 3, 94*)

Anne was born in Portland, and has a BFA from Oregon State University. In addition to her collaboration on the Lulu Award-winning *GoGirl!* with Trina Robbins, Anne's work includes the Eisner Award-nominated *Dignifying Science* and the comics version of *Star Trek: Deep Space Nine*. She has also drawn and painted children's books and covers and interior art for magazines including *Comic Book Artist* and *Wired*. She illustrated a poem in *Graphic Classics: Robert Louis Stevenson*, a comics version of *The Handsome Cabin Boy* for *Graphic Classics: Jack London*, and her art from the anthology *9-11 Artists Respond* is now included in the Library of Congress Collection. Samples of Anne's work are at www.homepage.mac.com/tafrin.

J. SHERIDAN LE FANU (*page 4*)

Joseph Thomas Sheridan Le Fanu was born in Dublin, Ireland in 1814. He was educated as a lawyer, but never practiced, instead opting for a career in journalism. He owned and edited several newspapers and magazines, but after the death of his wife in 1858 he became a recluse and devoted himself to the writing of supernatural horror tales. His *Carmilla* was published in 1872, twenty-five years before Bram Stoker's *Dracula*, on which he had an obvious influence. *Carmilla* has been filmed many times, under titles including *Blood and Roses, Tomb of the Vampire, The Vampire*

Lovers, *Lust for a Vampire* and *The Blood-Spattered Bride*.

ROD LOTT (*page 4*)

Oklahoma City resident Rod Lott is a freelance writer and graphic designer involved in advertising and journalism. For twelve years, he has published and edited the more-or-less quarterly magazine *Hitch: The Journal of Pop Culture Absurdity* (www.hitchmagazine.com), and recently started *Bookgasm*, a daily book review and news site at www.bookgasm.com. Rod's humorous essays have been published in several anthologies, including *May Contain Nuts* and *101 Damnations*. He has scripted comics adaptations of stories by Edgar Allan Poe, Clark Ashton Smith, Sax Rohmer, H.G. Wells, H.P. Lovecraft, O. Henry and Rafael Sabatini for *Graphic Classics*, and is now scripting a comics adaptation of Mary Shelley's *Frankenstein* for *Fantasy Classics*. You can learn more about Rod's work online at www.rodlott.com.

ANN RADCLIFFE (*page 44*)

Ann Radcliffe was one of the originators of, and certainly the most popular author of the gothic novel, a genre which featured fainting heroines, brooding heroes, haunted castles and spectral phenomena. Her epic novel *The Mysteries of Udolpho* (1794), has been called "the world's first best-seller," and she was one of the most popular and highly-paid authors of her time. Although she retired from writing early, her style would influence many writers including Mary Shelley, Sir Walter Scott, Jane Austen, the Brontë sisters and Edgar Allan Poe, who acknowledges her in his *The Oval Portrait*.

ANTONELLA CAPUTO (*page 44*)

Antonella was born and raised in Rome, Italy, and now lives in Lancaster, England. She has been an architect, archaeologist, art restorer, photographer, calligrapher, interior designer, theatre designer, actress and theatre director. Her first published work was *Casa Montesi*, a fortnightly comic strip which appeared in the national magazine *Il Giornalino*. She has since written comedies for children and scripts for comics and magazines in the UK, Europe and the U.S. She works with Nick Miller as the writing half of Team Sputnik, and has also collaborated with other artists in the *Graphic Classics* volumes *Edgar Allan Poe*, *Arthur Conan Doyle*, *H.G. Wells*, *Jack London*, *Ambrose Bierce*, *Mark Twain*, *O. Henry*, *Rafael Sabatini*, *Horror Classics* and *Adventure Classics*.

EDGAR ALLAN POE (*page 90*)

Edgar Allan Poe, the orphaned son of itinerant actors, led a tumultuous adolescence of drink and gambling, which resulted in the failure of both his university and military careers. Throughout his life he was plagued by poverty, poor health, insecurity, and depression, much by his own doing and a result of his continuing problems with alcohol. He struggled unsuccessfully as a writer until winning a short story contest in 1833. Poe's subsequent writing ranged from his rigorously metrical poetry to short stories, from journalism and distinguished literary criticism to the pseudo-scientific essays of *Eureka*. Today he is generally acknowledged as the inventor of both the gothic short story and the detective story, a pioneer of early science fiction and the founding father of the horror genre. He rightfully occupies the first volume in the *Graphic Classics* series, and a comics adaptation of Poe's *Some Words with a Mummy* appears in *Horror Classics: Graphic Classics Volume Ten*.

LEONG WAN KOK (*page 90*)

Leong Wan Kok, known to Malaysian comic readers as Puyuh, was born in Malaysia in the year of the rabbit. He now lives in Kuala Lumpur. Leong has been active in the comics industry in Malaysia since 2002, when he was invited to represent his country in the "Asia in Comics" festival in Tokyo. *The Oval Portrait* is his first work published in the U.S. He is now working on a comics adaptation of H.P. Lovecraft's *The Dream Quest of Unknown Kadath* for *Fantasy Classics*. In December 2006, his book of illustrations and comics, *Astro Cityzen*, was released in Malaysia. "This is a project that has taken seven months of my time and is my labor of love," says Leong. You can see more of his work online at www.1000tentacles.com.

TRINA ROBBINS (*page 94, back cover*)

Trina has been writing and drawing comics for more than thirty years, and since 1990 she has become a writer and feminist pop culture herstorian. Aside from her award-winning books on comics from a feminist perspective (*The Great Women Cartoonists* was listed among *Time Magazine's* top ten comics of 2001), she has written books about goddesses and murderesses, and she currently scripts *GoGirl!*, a teen superheroine comic illustrated by Anne Timmons. Trina and Anne also collaborated on *The Handsome Cabin Boy* for *Graphic Classics: Jack London*. While she has officially retired from drawing comics, Trina consented to contribute her illustration of *Northanger Abbey* for the back cover of this book. You can check out her website at www.trinarobbins.com.

MYLA JO CLOSSER (page 134)

Very little is known today about writer Myla Jo Closser, other than that she was born in 1880, was the wife of playwright Tarkington Baker, and the cousin of writer Booth Tarkington. *At the Gate* was originally published in *The Century Magazine*, and has been republished in numerous anthologies, including Emily Dorothy Scarborough's definitive *Famous Modern Ghost Stories*.

SHARY FLENNIKEN (page 134)

Shary Flenniken is a cartoonist, editor, author and screenwriter. She is best known for her irreverent comic strip *Trots & Bonnie*, about precocious preteens, which appeared in various underground comics and *National Lampoon*. Shary's graphic stories and comic strips have appeared in *Details*, *Premiere*, *Harvey*, and *Mad* magazines, as well as in *Graphic Classics: H.G. Wells*, *Graphic Classics: Ambrose Bierce*, *Graphic Classics: Mark Twain*, *Graphic Classics: Robert Louis Stevenson* and *Graphic Classics: O. Henry*. Her artwork can also be seen in *When a Man Loves A Walnut*, *More Misheard Lyrics* by the "very cool" Gavin Edwards, *Nice Guys Sleep Alone* by "big-time loser" Bruce Feirstein, and *Seattle Laughs*, a "truly wonderful" book edited by Shary. She is currently teaching comedy writing and cartooning while working on a book of fairy tales and a series of novels that she claims are "not even remotely autobiographical." You can contact Shary and find out how to purchase original artwork at www.sharyflenniken.com.

TOM POMPLUN

The designer, editor and publisher of the *Graphic Classics* series, Tom previously designed and produced *Rosebud*, a journal of poetry, fiction and illustration, from 1993 to 2003. He is now working on revised editions of *Graphic Classics: Bram Stoker* and *Graphic Classics: Mark Twain* as well as *Fantasy Classics*, a multi-author anthology to include works by Mary Shelley, Arthur Conan Doyle, L. Frank Baum and H.P. Lovecraft, with art by Michael Slack, Mark A. Nelson, Brad Teare, Simon Gane and Leong Wan Kok. You can find previews, sample art, and much more at www.graphicclassics.com.

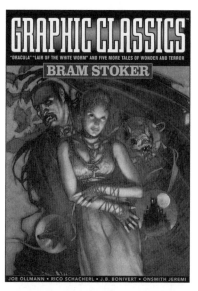

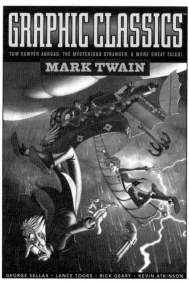